An F&F double: two Fabers,
two authors, two stories – *too much!*

Faber brings you a Honey O'Donahue Mystery
While Faber brings you a sizzling story of love on the run.

Honey Don't! and *Drive-Away Dykes!*

Two covers can barely contain the action!

About the Authors

JUAN CARLOS DAMIGO emigrated to Miami from his native Cuba in 1968, at the tender age of fifteen. Almost immediately Juan developed a love of 1970s variety television and learned to speak English through continuous viewings of the sketch comedy routines of Shields and Yarnell.

During these formative years Juan also developed a love of American literature by way of author Arthur Hailey. After graduating from Arkassippi Polytechnic, Juan published his first novel, *Too Much Love for One Man*, under the pen name Ethan Coen.

A former Kern County sheriff's deputy, and the law enforcement advisor for the hit NBC series *Police Woman*, TRICIA COOKE is also known for her hard-hitting activist journalism for the *LA Alt* and the *San Fernando Expat*. Tricia was the recipient of the 1972 Hal Fishman Award in Journalistic Excellence for her 1971 article, 'Doug Henning: It's not magic . . . it's cocaine.'

After meeting at an international conference on the lesbian antinomies of Immanuel Kant, Cooke and Damigo decided to team up for the first of their three literary collaborations, *Drive-Away Dykes*.

Damigo currently resides in Gorham, New Hampshire, with his four cats and a miniature potbelly pig named Peppers. Cooke resides in Millville, New Jersey.

Compiled by Stefan Dechant

DRIVE-AWAY DYKES

by the same authors

HONEY DON'T!

DRIVE-AWAY DYKES

The screenplay

ETHAN COEN AND TRICIA COOKE

faber

First published in 2025
by Faber & Faber Ltd
The Bindery, 51 Hatton Garden
London EC1N 8HN

First published in the USA in 2025

Typeset by Brighton Gray
Printed and bound by CPI Group (UK) Ltd, Croydon, CR0 4YY

A CIP record for this book is available from the British Library

ISBN 978-0-571-39912-3

Printed and bound in the UK on FSC® certified paper in line with our continuing commitment to ethical business practices, sustainability and the environment.

For further information see faber.co.uk/environmental-policy

Our authorised representative in the EU for product safety is
Easy Access System Europe, Mustamäe tee 50, 10621 Tallinn, Estonia
gpsr.requests@easproject.com

2 4 6 8 10 9 7 5 3 1

NEON SIGN: CICERO'S BAR AND GRILL.

The old neon sizzles.

INSIDE

We track slowly toward the back of the narrow, smoky room, bar to one side and booths to the other. A supered title sets the scene:

PHILADELPHIA
DECEMBER 1999

The booths' high wooden bench backs serve as partitions, giving privacy. Each booth we pass is empty until . . .

. . . the second-to-last. A man in a suit too fine for this working-class establishment peeks around from behind the partition. As we close in on him he looks apprehensively toward the bar's front door. His shoulders are oddly hunched.

He is suave but sweaty, wears tinted aviator glasses, has a thin mustache. A lock of black hair bounces rakishly over his forehead. He is Alejandro Santos.

He gives up on his look and swivels around to lean against the bench back. We match around.

Head-on now, we see what keeps his shoulders hunched: he's hugging an attaché case to his chest. On the table in front of him are a few empty wine glasses and an overflowing ashtray: he's been waiting here for some time. He looks at his watch.

His eyes shift fearfully up: someone stands before him, having approached without noise. Santos hugs the attaché case tighter, but . . .

It is only the waiter.

WAITER

Another glass of . . .

(*flicker of judgment*)

. . . rosé?

SANTOS

No!

Inhibited by the attaché case, he twists awkwardly for a last quick look toward the door, then looks back. His speech is lightly accented:

. . . The hour is long past.

(*he scribbles in the air*)

Check!

WILLIAM PENN STATUE

We are looking up at the statue atop Philadelphia's city hall. Though William Penn placidly smiles, the underlight lends him a sinister look.

STREET

We're pulling Santos, who walks hugging the attaché case. The Cicero's neon sign glows, out of focus, behind him. His breath vaporizes in the cold night air. The street is empty but Santos looks warily from side to side.

Someone emerges from the bar in the background. Focus is too soft for us to distinguish a face but we recognize the white of the waiter's apron.

In the foreground, Santos is unaware of the waiter who trots after him, pulling off his apron and tossing it to one side.

When the pursuing footsteps grow close enough to be heard, Santos looks back.

SANTOS

Ahgah!

He starts running.

The waiter too breaks into a run.

Santos turns down an alleyway.

ALLEY

Santos hugs the attaché case, panting as he corners.

He tips over a garbage pail at the alley mouth, lamely covering his retreat, and backs away, looking wildly about. It is a blind alley.

The waiter appears at the alley mouth. He gazes coolly in.

WAITER

The case, Santos.

SANTOS

My case! Stand back!

As he backs away:

. . . Do not advance!

The waiter steps over the tipped garbage pail and advances. He reaches up and slowly pulls one end of his waiter's bow tie until its knot tumbles loose.

WAITER

The case, Santos.

Santos grabs the lid off a tin garbage pail and holds it in front of himself as a shield.

SANTOS

Halt! Evil-doer!

Fingers wrap around the lid at three o'clock and nine o'clock, and with a sharp yank and a dull clung *it is wrenched from Santos's hand.*

The waiter sails the lid back over his head. It skids off an alley wall and clatters to the ground behind him. The waiter continues his advance, matching Santos's retreat step for step.

WAITER

The case, Santos.

SANTOS

Not on your life! *Waiter!*

The waiter pulls what looks like a jackknife from one pocket. He pries it open: a corkscrew.

Santos defensively raises the attaché case:

. . . Aahh!

With his free hand, the waiter sweeps the attaché case down. With his other hand he plunges the corkscrew into Santos's neck.

. . . AAAAHHHH!

Screaming, Alejandro Santos reaches up and tugs at the protruding cross-handle. The corkscrew remains embedded in his neck and his tugging at it only tents the skin outward.

. . . AAAAAHHHHH!

Still retreating, clutching the attaché case one-handed, Santos laboriously twists the corkscrew. Getting it out will be a long job.

Behind the waiter, at the mouth of the alley, a black car screeches to a halt. Its passenger door is flung open to disgorge a thug in a suit who trots toward us.

The waiter, oblivious, is pulling a ballpoint pen from his pocket. He transfers it to his left hand, raises it, clicks it, as Santos screams on:

. . . AAAAAHHHHHHH!

The waiter plunges the pen into the other side of Santos's neck. Its protruding angle complements the corkscrew's.

. . . AAAAAHHHHH!

Santos reaches with his other hand for the pen, dropping the attaché case as the man from the car arrives.

The waiter stoops, picks up the attaché case and, without looking, passes it back to the arriving thug, who immediately turns and runs it back toward the alley mouth.

The waiter reaches up and pats Santos gently on one cheek.

Santos's hands are both up at his own neck, clutching pen and corkscrew like handlebars that waggle his head.

. . . AAAAAAHHHHHHH!

The waiter's hand lingers on Santos's cheek. The thumb slides up under the glasses lens to press against the eye.

The other hand rises to the other cheek, thumb likewise sliding up against eyeball.

The waiter's grip on Santos's face tightens; the thumbs bear down.

Santos's head vibrates as he screams:

. . . AAAAHHHHH!

We cut discreetly to the alley mouth where the black car idles. The thug hands the attaché case in through the front passenger window and a hacksaw is handed out to him. Then the car screeches off. The man plunges back into the darkness of the alley, hacksaw in hand. Though we cannot see the gruesome doings within, the screams redouble, and, with a sting, the movie's title wipes on.

WILLIAM PENN STATUE

Smiling, uplit. The scream is now distant.

A DARK APARTMENT HALLWAY

The scream is louder here. But wait: this is a different scream, coming from inside a bedroom down the hall.

THE BEDROOM

The scream – a woman's scream – is louder still:

WOMAN

AAAAHHHH!

The woman is staring up in close shot, screaming.

Wider shows her in bed, under a sheet which, below her waist, bips and bops and jiffy-pops with the action of her partner's head.

The ring of a phone. The beep of an answering machine.

OUTGOING MESSAGE

Neither Sukie nor Jamie are here right now. Leave a message.

WOMAN

AAAHHHHH!

A beep. A woman's voice:

CALLER

Jamie, it's me.

WOMAN

OH MY GOD! JAMIE!

CALLER

Are you there?

The woman's partner whips the sheet off her head – another young woman. She stares into space, listening, as the woman beneath her continues to writhe. From the machine:

. . . Are you coming tonight?

WOMAN

AH, PLEASE!

CALLER

Let me know because I'm not going to this . . . *thing*, if you're not.

WOMAN

JAMIE!

CALLER

I won't know anyone. I mean I guess Diane'll be there.

WOMAN

JAMIE! JAMIE! JAMIE!

CALLER

But I don't want to be stuck there talking to Diane. Maybe Carla will be there.

WOMAN

OH!

Despairing of her partner, the woman starts rubbing herself.

CALLER

Do you know if Carla's going? Call me and let me know.

WOMAN

AAAHHHH!

Jamie looks at her masturbating partner.

JAMIE

Are you going?

CARLA

AAAAHHH! PLEASE!

CALLER

Anyway. Call me if you would.

CARLA

OH MY GOD!

CALLER

(*suddenly suspicious*)

. . .You're not there, are you?

OFFICE

The caller listens briefly at the telephone, then hangs up. Her dress is businesslike, even prim: neat suit, collar buttoned to the neck.

A young man in shirtsleeves and tie drapes an arm over her cubicle's partition.

MAN

Hey! Marian!

MARIAN

Hi, Bart.

She gives him an icy smile. He responds to the smile and is oblivious to its reserve.

BART

. . . Say – what're you doing tomorrow night? There's a Phish concert.

MARIAN

. . . What?

BART

Phish concert. Great jam band. At the civic center.

MARIAN

Yeah, oh, I . . .

BART

P-H.

MARIAN
(*tart*)
I know how to spell Phish.

BART
Yeah, course. I –

MARIAN
I'm sorry, I have an engagement.

BART
Okay, bummer. Didn't mean to, you know.

MARIAN
It's fine.

BART
Yeah, sure. Anyhoo. What about –

MARIAN
Please don't use that expression.

BART
What expression.

MARIAN
'Anyhoo.'

BART
It's not an expression.

MARIAN
What is it.

BART
A word.

MARIAN
Please don't use that word.

BART
Okay. You free Wednesday?

MARIAN
Plus, it isn't even a word. Not really.

BART

Okay, sure. Free for dinner Wednesday? There's a new place near me, Montana's, it's very good. Yeah, it's trendy, but the food is super-gourmet. American regional. It's really very –

MARIAN

No, I have an engagement Wednesday.

BART

Okay. Huh. Wednesday too.

(*beat*)

People don't usually call them 'engagements.'

MARIAN

Do *I* tell *you* how to speak?

BART

. . . Yes.

MARIAN

The fact remains.

BART

The engagement.

MARIAN

That's right.

Beat.

BART

Is it a fact? The engagement?

MARIAN

What if it weren't, Bart? What would I be saying to you if it *weren't* a fact, if I *didn't* really have an engagement?

BART

I guess you'd be telling me to, um . . .

MARIAN

That's right. That's exactly right.

DARKENED APARTMENT

Close on Jamie who faces the headboard, bucking, astraddle her friend's face.

JAMIE

OH MY GOD! OH MY GOD!

The phone rings.

WOMAN

Nnngh!

JAMIE

OH MY GOD!

OUTGOING MESSAGE

Neither Sukie nor Jamie are –

JAMIE

OH MY – Mmmhff . . . GODDAMNIT!

She flops off and swipes up the bedside phone.

. . . Jesus, Marian, *don't* call me during sex, *yes* I'm going to shot night!

Beat. She quickly sobers.

. . . Oh. Hi Sukie.

OFFICE

Marian listens briefly to a busy signal, then hangs up.

APARTMENT

Close on Jamie, still on the phone, the cloud of panic having fully darkened her sweaty face. The bed she sits on continues to joggle and squeak, agitated by her companion offscreen.

JAMIE

Who? *Here?* No one's *here*. I was masturbating.

(*casts about for the phrase*)

. . . *Me* time.

A scream from the bed. Jamie's look stays focused at a point in space.

. . . Lemme turn down the video.

NEON SIGN: SUGAR'N SPICE

Music pulses within the club.

INSIDE

Loud music. Marian, at the bar, still wears what we saw her in at work, which is more formal than anything worn by the rest of the lesbian bar's clientele.

VOICE

No.

Marian looks at the accuser offscreen.

MARIAN

What.

VOICE

No.

Marian gives a what-are-you-talking-about shrug.

MARIAN

No what, Carla?

A reverse shows that it is indeed Carla, the woman Jamie was having sex with.

CARLA

You're not wearing that.

Another shrug from Marian.

MARIAN

I came from work.

CARLA

I came from Toledo, I don't *dress* like it.

MARIAN

Is Jamie here?

Carla wedges in to the bar next to Marian, appraising her wardrobe.

CARLA

Okay look. Leave the coat on, just get rid of the shirt underneath.

Marian looks down at her pantsuit coat's widely separated lapels, looks back up.

MARIAN

And flaunt my breasts? I'm not here to peddle my wares.

Carla gives a quick look around the raucous bar. Back to Marian:

CARLA

Why else would you be here?

MARIAN

(*starchy*)

To *socialize.*

CARL

(*deadpan*)

Okay.

The music cuts out as a public-address system sputters on:

AMPLIFIED VOICE

Hello, girls, all I hear lately is, Y2K, Y2K – but Jamie Dobbs is here to say –

There are cheers as we cut to the stage where the DJ tips her mike to Jamie, just mounting the little bandstand.

JAMIE

– Why *not* 2K!

Cheers from the crowd, arm-waved on by Jamie.

. . . New millenium, bring it on!

More cheers; the DJ reclaims the microphone.

DJ

It's the last body-shot competition of 1999 here at Sugar and Spice and Jamie is last month's winner so we are gonna SALT you UP!

(*cheers*)

Show us where the first lick goes, babe.

Jamie wets a finger and dips it in a small silver bowl.

JAMIE

Right . . . here!

She applies the salt to the hollow of her throat, to warm applause.

ANGRY VOICE

God, look at that slut.

A woman is standing at Marian's shoulder, her burning look fixed on Jamie.

MARIAN

Hi Sukie.

As she talks to Marian, Sukie's glare stays fixed on the stage:

SUKIE

Don't put that woman in front of a *crowd*. With a *microphone* for god's sake.

MARIAN

Well. She likes to entertain.

We hear Jamie, off:

JAMIE

Second lick . . . here!

Warmer applause and cheers. Sukie takes in the crowd's reaction.

SUKIE

And then she gets this *reinforcement*. Do you know who she's fucking?

MARIAN

I don't know that she's seeing anyone. She's seeing *you*, of course.

JAMIE

(*off*)

Third lick . . . *here*!

Wild cheers.

MARIAN

She's a free spirit, I admire her.

Sukie gives a sharp, mirthless hoot.

SUKIE

Free, yeah, that's the problem. Put a meter on her pussy we could all retire.

MARIAN

Oh that's not fair, Susanne. It's –

JAMIE

(*off*)

And a LIME WEDGE . . . *HERE*!

Eyes widening as they watch Jamie, off:

MARIAN

Oh!

SUKIE

OH!

Ecstatic cheers from the crowd. We hold on Marian as Sukie leaves frame, yelling:

. . . PULL THAT OUT! THAT IS NOT A PUBLIC RECEPTACLE!

Marian and Carla both stare at the offscreen march-away. Carla murmurs a sing-songy:

CARLA

Someone's gonna get hi-i-i-it.

The words are punctuated by an impact sound and crowd reaction.

MARIAN'S APARTMENT

Later. Close on Jamie, who's sitting back in an armchair pressing a baggie of frozen peas against one eye.

JAMIE

I have had it with L-O-V-E love. I know bards 'n' troubadours are high on it but I don't believe it's relevant to the modern twentieth-soon-to-be-twenty-first-century lesbian.

MARIAN

Here's some carrots. Those peas are thawed.

She has entered from the kitchen with a bag of frozen carrots, which Jamie takes and applies.

JAMIE

This right here is what it gets you. So I have hatched a plan, my friend. If you'll help me move my shit out of Sukie's tomorrow –

MARIAN

I'm not getting in the middle of that. I have my own problems.

JAMIE

What problems.

MARIAN
(*tight-lipped*)

Internal.

JAMIE

Internal.

MARIAN

Problems with what I *feel*. Internally.

JAMIE

Like anal beads? How can you have internal problems, you got your ass bricked up.

She absently tears open the bag of peas in her lap and picks them out one at a time to chew on.

I am not certain, honey-darlin, that you have *ever* reached deep inside a *any* orifice to scoop out your soul and fling it shamelessly at a fellow human being and humiliate yourself 'n' grovel 'n' weep 'n' feel yer ego completely disintegrate, otherwise known as the Glory of Love.

MARIAN

Please don't eat those peas.

JAMIE

Now m'*plan* is, you help me pack my stuff 'n' then we two –

MARIAN

I can't. I'm leaving town.

JAMIE

What! I am too, that was my plan! Where *you* goin?

MARIAN

Tallahassee, Florida.

Jamie stares at her.

JAMIE

Death in the family?

MARIAN

Not at all. My –

JAMIE

Why else would anyone go to Tallahassee Florida?

MARIAN

My Aunt Ellis is there.

Another stare from Jamie.

JAMIE

Can't she move?

MARIAN

Tallahassee is very nice. It's not glitzy and gross like Miami, it has live oak and Spanish moss. Me and Aunt Ellis go to the St. Mark's Wildlife Preserve, there's good birding.

JAMIE

Birding. How've I missed out on this.

MARIAN

It's very pleasant.

JAMIE

So you just came up with this plan. To bird.

MARIAN

It didn't just come up. It's been growing.

JAMIE

This wild hair 'n' your ass, to bird.

MARIAN

I've been unhappy and I'm starting to snap at people at work and it's not fair to them because I'm only unhappy with myself.

JAMIE

Well we can *fix* that! We'll have you runnin' right in no time, that's why we take this trip together, honey-babe. We get our shit together, together. See, I was gonna take some time off too, get a drive-away, just go pot-luck anywhere – and now you can come with me! And we get to go to Tallahassee! And *bird*!

MARIAN

What's a drive-away?

JAMIE

It's a free one-way rental. You deliver the car to where some client of the drive-away company wants it, if they got one goin' near your destination.

MARIAN

I don't know if you'll like Aunt Ellis.

JAMIE

Are you kidding? A *birder*? I'll wear my great big straw hat! And she is gonna love L-O-V-E *love* me! *You* know how parents 'n' such love me, they think I got charisma, 'Oh Marian, who's your loquacious friend I love that chatty little girl isn't she just *some*thing!'

MARIAN

I'm not sure I –

JAMIE

Don't go finding a problem here, this is gonna be f-u-n-n *funn*, girl. Just come help me pack up tomorrow – don't worry, Sukie's not gonna be there.

SUKIE

Loudly weeping. Her and Jamie's apartment.

In the background, Jamie and Marian stand awkwardly by. Neither knows what to say. Jamie holds a box piled with her belongings.

Sukie is seated on the floor, unscrewing something from the wall as she sobs and sobs. A loud yapping comes from somewhere in the room.

SUKIE

Oh god! Take it! Oh god!

The angle on Marian and Jamie shows the leaping, excited schnauzer, source of the insistent yapping.

JAMIE

Sukie, don't. What're you doing.

Mucous bubbles and saliva dribbles as Sukie weeps:

SUKIE

Take it! Take it! I don't *want* it anymore!

Marian hisses at Jamie:

MARIAN

You said she wouldn't be here.

JAMIE

Sukie, I'm just taking my own stuff. That was a gift. I wanted *you* to have it.

The plate Sukie is unscrewing from the wall anchors an uptilted phallus.

SUKIE

I! Don't! Want it! If we're not going to both! Use it!

JAMIE

Sukie, it's *your* wall-dildo.

SUKIE

No! No! No! No! And take Alice, too! I never liked her!

JAMIE

How can I take the dog, Sukie – I don't have a home. Remember, you kicked me out?

SUKIE

(*sobbing*)

Take Alice!

JAMIE

I'm going on a road trip –

SUKIE

Take Alice! Take the wall-dildo!

MARIAN

(*soothing*)

It's your dildo, Susanne.

DRIVE-AWAY INTERIOR

It is a run-down street-fronting establishment. CURLIE'S DRIVE-AWAY is painted on its front window.

In the foreground, a grizzled and balding man is on the phone. His work shirt has a name patch sewn on: CURLIE. Behind Curlie, through the window, we see a cab pulling up and Marian and Jamie getting out, Jamie juggling her piled-high box atop which the wall-dildo wobbles.

CURLIE

Curlie's Drive-Away, Pennsylvania's most trusted name in car delivery, Curlie speaking . . . Uh-huh. Tallahassee, Florida . . . Yes I'm writing it down.

He is not writing anything down.

. . . Right . . . Sure . . . Right . . . Got it.

Jamie and Marian have entered. Jamie drops her box on the counter that separates them from Curlie.

JAMIE

Can you help us?

Curlie, without looking, holds up a finger: one second. He listens at the phone.

CURLIE

. . . By tomorrow . . . Uh-huh . . . Okay.

He hangs up.

JAMIE

Can you help us? We want a drive-away.

CURLIE

Two-hundred-fifty-dollar deposit and a reference.

JAMIE

A reference?

CURLIE

Somebody local I can break his balls you don't show up where you're supposed to.

MARIAN

Break his – can the reference be a woman?

JAMIE

We don't know a lot of men.

The man looks, deadpan, at the dildo atop Jamie's belongings.

CURLIE

No kiddin'.

MARIAN

We're very good drivers.

JAMIE

Licensed.

Curlie stares at her. She adds, lamely:

. . . By the state.

Curlie draws a card file across the desktop.

CURLIE

Where you wanna go.

MARIAN

Tallahassee.

This brings his look up.

CURLIE

Tallahassee?

MARIAN

What's wrong with Tallahassee? It's very nice, there's Spanish moss and –

JAMIE

I think Curlie is just surprised that –

CURLIE

Don't call me Curlie.

JAMIE

Isn't your name Curlie?

CURLIE

My name is Curlie. We just met. It's too familiar.

MARIAN

Have you ever *been* to Tallahassee?

CURLIE

No, I got good sense. Your car is a Dodge Aries.

MARIAN

Oh.

(*surprised it's so easy*)

Okay, is that a good car?

CURLIE

Not really.

JAMIE

You sell those shirts?

A LARGE FOLD-OUT MAP

On Marian's kitchen table. A hand with a black pen marks sites between Philadelphia and Tallahassee.

JAMIE'S VOICE

There's also a place here in Wilmington, fantastic dyke bar, the Butter Churn, and this place Levi's Barbecue in Charleston –

The black pen, having written DYKES! next to Wilmington, North Carolina, procedes to write BBQ next to Charleston.

– Memphis-style barbecue, really good, everyone goes to Charlie Vergos' but –

MARIAN'S VOICE

Jamie!

Another hand enters with a highlighter to – squeeeak – *trace the length of the interstate, Highway 95, down to Jacksonville, then over to Tallahassee.*

. . . It's a straight shot to Tallahassee. *Down* . . . and *across*.

The hand with the black pen marks another site not near the interstate.

JAMIE'S VOICE

Right here's the world's largest Dixie Cup, in Mitchell, Georgia –

The pen has written DIXIE CUP but the highlighter hand re-enters.

MARIAN'S VOICE

Direct route. *Down* . . . and *across*. We don't need to see the world's largest Dixie Cup.

The black pen circles Dixie Cup once, twice, for emphasis.

JAMIE'S VOICE

We don't need to enjoy life, but as long as we're here . . .

MARIAN'S VOICE

The world's largest Dixie Cup is not 'life.' It's a straight shot on the interstate. *Down* . . . and *across*.

JAMIE'S VOICE

The *interstate* is not 'life.'

MARIAN'S VOICE

It is, more than the world's largest Dixie Cup.

JAMIE'S VOICE

You're the one who wanted to go birding!

MARIAN'S VOICE

That's *nature*!

JAMIE'S VOICE

What's a *dyke* bar? That's not *nature*? Even a Dixie Cup, you could make an *argument*!

MARIAN

He said it was a rush job. We're supposed to have the car there *tomorrow*.

With a hollow, wubbling sound against the wood table underneath, the black pen underlines the map's three marked destinations.

JAMIE

Tomorrow can wait a day! Attractions! We could even go to Miami! *South* Beach! Bikinis 'n' high heels!

CURLIE'S

Curlie is on the phone. Through the storefront window we see the approach of two men in cheap suits.

CURLIE

. . . A medical doctor? . . . Oh, a *reverend*. Yeah, no we don't have a discount for men a' god, no . . . No, not for medical doctors either – make up your mind, which *are* you?

The men enter. The larger man is Flint. The smaller is Arliss. Curlie holds up a finger: one second.

. . . No we don't have *any* discounts, our everyday prices are already rock-bottom. Thank you for calling Curlie's Drive-Away, Pennsylvania's most trusted name in car delivery.

He hangs up.

FLINT

Well. We're here.

CURLIE

You're here. Who're you.

FLINT

The car.

CURLIE

The car.

FLINT

The Dodge Aries.

Curlie stares.

CURLIE

The Dodge Aries.

FLINT

What're you, a myna bird?

CURLIE

I'm Curlie.

FLINT

I understand that.

CURLIE

You're not the Dodge.

FLINT

What do you mean, we're not the Dodge.

CURLIE

. . . *You're* the Dodge? Talla*hassee*?

EARTHQUAKE TRANSITION (the outgoing frame shakes violently with rumble effect)

TO THE DODGE

Painted on its trunk in cheerful dayglo colors: LOVE IS A SLEIGH RIDE TO HELL.

INTERIOR

Marian drives.

JAMIE

What's the big deal?

MARIAN

The car isn't *ours*!

JAMIE

But it's *art*! And the car *is* ours, till Tallahassee.

MARIAN

And once we get to Tallahassee it stops being 'art' and starts being vandalism.

JAMIE

Well for fickety-fuck's sake, Marian, it'll come off with a little soap and water – transformer!

MARIAN

Huh?

Jamie points up at a passing power line.

JAMIE

Electrical transformer.

MARIAN

It won't.

JAMIE

Won't what.

MARIAN

Come off with soap and water.

JAMIE

How do you know?

MARIAN

I tried.

JAMIE

Marian! It's *art*!

MARIAN

Stop saying it's *art*, that doesn't end all discussion. We're going to be driving through some conservative towns. The South? The Bible Belt?

JAMIE

Don't I know it! Honey, I grew up where the Bible Belt meets the ass-crack of the Pecos River.

MARIAN

Fort Worth is nowhere near the Pecos River.

(*pronounces it 'pay-coze'*)

JAMIE

That's Peck-us, honey-darlin'. And the car art is just part of my larger *undertaking*. My *project*.

MARIAN

What's your project?

JAMIE

Loosening you up so we can get you laid, sugar-sweet. How long's it been?

MARIAN

Well – I don't know . . .

JAMIE

Weeks? Months?

Silence.

. . . Oh my god, Marian, don't tell me it's been years? How many years? Who was it? It wasn't – you've had sex since what's-her-name, haven't you?

MARIAN
(*tight*)

Donna.

JAMIE

Yeah, Donna.

She looks at Marian. Silence.

. . . Ohmygod. Ohmygod, *Donna*. She's working for Al Gore now?

MARIAN
(*tight*)

Nader.

JAMIE

Oh, that's right, she just looks like Al Gore. When you broke up, who got the stick?

MARIAN

What stick?

JAMIE

The one you both had up your ass?

GO-GIRL TRANSITION (*spinning revolving door with whizzing-car-by effect*).

TO CURLIE'S DRIVE-AWAY

Arliss and Flint have been joined by a third man, in a better suit, an apparently senior Chief.

CURLIE

You said people of yours would come for it.

CHIEF

I said people would come for it.

CURLIE

You call with the drop-off in Tallahassee and these broads come in and say they're ready to go to Tallahassee.

CHIEF

I see. You're an idiot.

CURLIE

Could be.

ARLISS

You gave them the car; you don't know who they were.

CURLIE

I told you their names.

CHIEF

Their names, yes, but –

FLINT

This place is a dump.

CURLIE

They drive the car instead of you. Is that bad?

CHIEF

Bad if they find the, goods.

FLINT

This place is a pigsty. Why don't you get a girl in?

CURLIE

I like clutter.

CHIEF

They didn't have a cellphone?

CURLIE

Sterile doesn't work for me.

FLINT

He asked you a question, dick-yank!

CHIEF

Flint –

CURLIE

Dick-yank? *I'm* a dick-yank?

CHIEF

Flint, please, don't antagonize.

Curlie and Flint are locked in male-hatred eye contact.

FLINT

It's like talking to a bucket of wet cement!

CURLIE

You wouldn't know wet cement if it bit you in the ass.

FLINT

And you would?

CHIEF

So there's no way to get in touch with them.

CURLIE

(*eyes still locked on Flint*)

Not per se.

FLINT

'Per se'?!

Curlie turns from Flint in dismissal and addresses the Chief.

CURLIE

They left a contact. Everybody's gotta leave a local contact. Somebody whose balls I can break if – ugh!

Arliss, behind him, has just smacked him on the head with a billy club.

Curlie drops the paperwork he has just dug out. A sheet of paper dipsy-doodles toward the floor.

Curlie touches his head, looks at the blood on his hand.

CURLIE

Now you've gone and done it.

The Chief squats and snags the paper out of the air.

Curlie swipes a scissors off the desk and turns to Arliss, raising it.

Flint punches him in the kidney.

The Chief rises, looking at the paper. His knees crack.

CHIEF

Mhh.

Curlie has sunk to one side with kidney pain. Arliss again cracks him over the head. Flint gives him another kidney punch.

The two men beat him to the floor. They begin kicking him.

The Chief looks down his nose, through bifocals, at the paper. As the sounds of the beating continue, off, he murmurs:

. . . Well, Susanne Shinkleman . . . 1418 Chestnut Street . . .

He gazes thoughtfully at the beating.

. . . You'd better hope your friends deliver that car. Tomorrow.

EARTHQUAKE TRANSITION TO:

CHEAP MOTEL ROOM

The girls enter a depressing motel room. Jamie flings a backpack onto the moth-eaten bedspread and drinks in the ambience.

JAMIE

This is great. This is so slutty. I love this. I hope they have postcards.

MARIAN

Jamie –

JAMIE

All right, let's put on our warpaint; the Butter Churn awaits.

MARIAN

Jamie, I think I'd prefer to –

JAMIE

No. No. Don't even. You come with me. I'm gonna show you how this is done.

SEEDY OFFICE

The horrible motel office has a horrible Formica front desk behind which sits a horrible old man. The rest of the room is something in the nature of a horrible lounge, consisting of a much-spilled-upon sofa that faces a television set tuned to a horrible sitcom.

The girls enter.

JAMIE

Hiya, do you know where the Butter Churn is? It's a dyke bar?

The old man looks at her, deadpan, or perhaps vegetative.

. . . Or do you have like a *Time Out Wilmington*? I mean is there one? With gay/lesbian listings?

The old man stares.

. . . I mean *you* wouldn't have it; is there a newsstand? Or a lesbian bookstore, you know, 'Sapphic Wonders,' something like that?

The old man stares.

. . . Hello? Do the words I am speaking mean anything to you at all.

EXTERIOR

The drive-away car's trunk with its painted-on slogan, LOVE IS A SLEIGH RIDE TO HELL, glides into bird's-eye view as the car pulls into frame and stops.

On a double-clunk of opening doors we cut laterally. The two women emerge. They look at the Butter Churn across the street. Loud music thuds within.

JAMIE

You have to show that you're comfortable with the physical.

Her own body language is as fluid as a hula dancer's.

. . . This isn't like, meeting someone at a NOW convention where you talk about dismantling the patriarchy.

MARIAN

Jamie, I've done this before.

JAMIE

It's just, like, one message: you dig the female body. *Your* body. You're like this.

(*hula movement*)

You're not like –
(*drawing herself up to full height, lowering her voice*)
Let's dismantle the patriarchy.

MARIAN

I have done this before. I am not a schoolmarm.

JAMIE

You fuck people who work for Ralph Nader!

MARIAN

Not *only*.

JAMIE

Only in the last four years!

MARIAN

Three years.

(*beat*)

And four months. And fourteen days.

INTERIOR BUTTER CHURN

The two women enter and look around, Marian frowning, Jamie clinical, her head bopping with the music.

JAMIE

. . . Okay, diggin' your body?

MARIAN

(*defensive*)

Very much so!

JAMIE

Okay! And who looks good to you?

Marian looks around.

MARIAN

They all look fine.

JAMIE

Fine? Like, *you'll* do? Please, please come home with me, baby, you seem totally okay? Are there any other mediocre ones like you at home?

MARIAN

I didn't say they all looked *mediocre*, I said they all looked *fine*.

JAMIE

But not in the sense of Supa-Fine, in the sense of Fine, Whatever.

MARIAN

Why are you jousting with me?

JAMIE

I'm not *jousting*, I'm asking which of these women you wanna throw up against the wall and fuck like there's no tomorrow.

MARIAN

Look. Jamie. I am not a throw-against-the-wall-and-fuck-the-daylights-out-of kind of person. Stop trying to make me something I'm not.

JAMIE

I'm just trying to get you laid! They *sense* it, whether you want to fuck them or you just think they're *fine*.

MARIAN

I have to be *me*. It has to be done with *authenticity.*

JAMIE

You mean with *authority*.

MARIAN

I mean with *authenticity*.

JAMIE

Authenticity gets you someone who works for Ralph Nader.

MARIAN

You don't know what our life was like! You know nothing of its *worth*!

JAMIE

Then why didn't the two of you move to Santa Fe and synchronize your menstrual cycles? That didn't *happen*! That's why you're here in a *dyke* bar, looking for cheap sleazy sex!

MARIAN

No. I'm not.

(*she stands*)

This is not me. You're right, I can't do this.

As Marian starts to go:

JAMIE

No, Marian, I'm sorry, honey-girl, I'm saying you *can* do this. You can *do* this! You can be cheap! I promise you you can, honey-darlin'! Your best self!

MARIAN

Jamie, I know you're well intentioned but this really isn't right for me. You should stay and enjoy your night on the town.

As she watches Marian go, Jamie breathes the words:

JAMIE

'On the town'?

MOTEL ROOM

Marian is propped up in bed, reading.

The book: Henry James' The Europeans.

Back to Marian reading. A noise brings her look up.

The door. We hear scratches and scrapes at it. And giggling.

Back to Marian. Eyes on the door.

Back to the door. More scrapes ending with a ka-thunk *of a key finally making it into the lock. A short beat. Then the sound of the key turning and the door is pushed and – doesn't move.*

Marian sets the book aside, hesitates, throws off covers, prepares to rise –

The door. The key is turned the other way and the door is pushed open to reveal Jamie and another woman. Jamie is delayed at the door as she tries to extract the key, turning it this way and that, swaying and giggling.

The other woman, who has stumbled into the room, comes up short looking at Marian in bed.

WOMAN

Hello.

MARIAN

. . . Good evening.

WOMAN

I'm Amber.

MARIAN
(*tight*)

Marian.

AMBER

. . . Wutcha readin?

MARIAN

The Europeans. By Henry James.

AMBER

Wow. Thick one.

Jamie has finally gotten the key out.

JAMIE

Hello Marian.

MARIAN

Hello.

Amber's look travels between the two.

AMBER

So . . . Is this gonna be a threesome?

MARIAN

No!

JAMIE

Nooo, no.

AMBER

Oh. Okay. Rats.

MARIAN

Well . . .

She starts out of bed.

. . . I'll just . . .

OFFICE

The TV in the horrible motel office. A syndicated sitcom plays, too loudly.

The motel manager. He sits stubbly jaw agape, head cocked and his look steeply angled up toward the TV.

Marian. She sits on the horrible sofa in an overcoat and galoshes and bra and underwear, reading The Europeans. *Or anyway staring at the open book, trying to read.*

FADE OUT.

IN BLACK

Sound from the inane sitcom has cross-faded into distant, reverb-heavy acid rock of late-sixties vintage. Strangely, the sitcom's roaring laugh track has not faded. It punctuates the rock music with intermittent, eerily unmotivated laughs.

Music and laughter cut to loud car tone as we go to:

THE DODGE

Jamie drives, Marian rides.

MARIAN

. . . How was it?

A beat.

JAMIE

Bouncy.

Silence. Driving.

Jamie looks at Marian.

. . . How's your book?

MARIAN

Good. It's about two . . . free spirits who visit a repressed family in New England.

JAMIE

Well hello, they're all repressed in New England. That's why we're going the other way. Although there was this one chick I screwed once from New Hampshire? She got her tongue so far in me I thought it was gonna wriggle out my asshole.

Driving. Marian doesn't react.

. . . No, I'm not kidding.

More driving.

. . . They say there are advanced yoga people who can do that. In India, supposedly. Black belts in cunnilingus, which is a hell of a word in my opinion. They can even cunniling themselves, they have pictures of it in, like, medical books. Ya gotta ask the librarian, they don't keep 'em in the stacks.

More driving.

. . . Who wrote *your* book?

MARIAN

Henry James.

JAMIE

Henry James.

MARIAN

American writer? Famous family? His brother, too –

JAMIE

Rick?

MARIAN

Uh . . .

JAMIE

No, I'm kiddin', I know who Henry James is. White and uptight. They made us read *Portrait of a Lady* in school. Boy, that was a great read. Like someone dragging day-old spaghetti across my tits.

MARIAN

That's a very apt simile. His writing is labyrinthine. And clammy.

JAMIE

Yeah, it put me off the whole book thing. Henry James is, in fact, the reason I don't read.

MARIAN

Uh-huh.

JAMIE

Except road signs.

MARIAN

Uh-huh, yeah, I don't think you should've brought someone back to the room.

A conversation derailer. After a beat:

JAMIE

Okay, I knew this was comin'.

MARIAN

How do you think I felt?

JAMIE

You told me to have a night on the town!

MARIAN

People say things, it's not always what they feel.

JAMIE

Well I'm from Texas, I don't read minds, we operate on a handshake basis.

MARIAN

What does *that* mean?

JAMIE

Hey there, how ya doin', how much for this Cadillac car, how'd ya like to have oral sex? *Texas*.

MARIAN

Okay.

JAMIE

Where *you* from, girl?

MARIAN

Not Texas!

JAMIE

I know that!

MARIAN

Then why'd you ask?

JAMIE

BECAUSE I –

The anger hits a wall along with the thought. After a beat, quietly:

. . . I'm sorry.

Another beat.

MARIAN

No, *I'm* sorry.

JAMIE

For *what*, you're okay, you're *good*, I'm a little –

MARIAN

Nah, I'm a big baby sometimes, I –

JAMIE

UNCLE GINO'S!

EXTERIOR

The screech of tires stings the cut as the car cuts sharply into the highway's exit lane.

INTERIOR UNCLE GINO'S PIZZA

A rest-stop restaurant. Jamie brings a tray to Marian, already seated.

JAMIE

You are not going to believe this. See over there?

Marian looks.

Across the room, at several tables pushed together, is a boisterous party of a dozen ponytailed young women wearing numbered jerseys and short pleated dresses. They are aglow with health and fitness.

. . . Girls' soccer team. I was in line next to Doreen, the captain.

MARIAN

Uh-huh.

JAMIE

They're very committed lesbians and they're on their way to Marietta, Georgia, which is practically on our way.

MARIAN

Not exactly. We were supposed to deliver the car today – should we look at the map, see how long –

JAMIE

Life isn't on the map, I thought we agreed! And after tonight's game they're having a basement party. And guess who's invited.

MARIAN

I'm sure *you* are.

JAMIE

Nuh-uh. *Us!* Ya see? Shit happens when y'eat at Uncle Gino's.

EARTHQUAKE TRANSITION TO:

LIGHT SHOW

It is a moving abstraction of writhing amoeba-like blobs in dayglo colors. The sixties acid rock we've heard before returns, blaring.

Bending shapes – shadows – silhouettes – of human beings? – pass before the whirling colors. Talking, smoking, laughing: a party of some kind?

Through the wall of noise, an insistent ring, a telephone, growing louder and louder but its tone oddly dulled and tied to a rattling sound.

HARD CUT TO:

CURLIE

We're close on him. Somewhere a phone rings, the ring dully rattling.

Curlie lies with one cheek resting on the floor, his face battered. He stares at us semi-sightlessly through drooping lids, moaning softly.

The floor is covered with papers and smashed office effects. Feet enter behind Curlie to wade through the wreckage, and then hands enter as someone bends to swipe through the papers, searching.

The ringing is suddenly sharper as papers that had covered a telephone – and were rattled by its ringer – are swatted away. The phone is lifted out of frame.

We cut up as the Chief puts the phone on a countertop and uncradles it.

CHIEF

Hello? . . . They didn't . . . That's all right, we've got a Plan B . . . Yes, sir . . . I understand that, sir . . .

He takes out a handkerchief to wipe his brow. He is getting his ass chewed out.

. . . Yes, sir, you have my word on it. And let me just –

He reacts to a hang-up.

He cradles the phone. He looks up.

Arliss and Flint lounge at the storefront window that still holds fading dusk. Arliss idly twirls his billy club. Both men look to the Chief for news.

. . . No-show.

A FINISHED BASEMENT

We are slowly panning the classic finished basement done in cheap paneling and wall-to-wall carpet and a low dropped ceiling of Johnson-Armstrong tile. There is a paneled bar with pink-upholstered white plastic bar stools and a home-entertainment center with hi-fi, which is the source of the soulful Linda Ronstadt song that enters at the cut.

Every sofa and chair in the room is occupied by a pair of girls, necking.

We pan the long, languorous make-out kisses, the hand of many a girl groping under her partner's jersey or pleated skirt.

The pan finally brings us on to someone not in uniform: Jamie, enthusiastically making out with the soccer girl in her lap.

The continuing pan brings us off of them and on to Marian, necking more self-consciously as she sits in the lap of a larger girl – the goalie, perhaps.

The song fades to silence, leaving only the rhythmic thud of needle against groove-end, and a few soft, ongoing moans.

Doreen, the captain of the team, clears her throat.

DOREEN

Okay. Rotate right.

One girl from each pair stands and shuffles to the new partner on her right.

This leaves Marian standing in front of the seated Jamie.

Jamie smiles at Marian.

Marian is frozen, mortified. She finally stammers to the room:

MARIAN

Um . . . Can we . . . see, actually, we're just friends . . .

The girls stare at her, each couple arrested in the course of arranging itself to make out.

Doreen stares, holding the tone-arm of the record player frozen over a spinning disk.

Twenty-two staring eyes. Seven ponytails. Eight pigtails.

Jamie waggles Marian's hand and hisses:

JAMIE

Come on, Marian, it's no big deal!

Now only more mortified, Marian sits into Jamie's lap. Another song starts up.

Marian and Jamie feel awkwardly for places to fit their hands.

Jamie laughs self-consciously.

Eyes wide, Marian leans slowly in.

Her lips meet Jamie's as Linda Ronstadt begins a new song.

A HAND RAPPING AT A DOOR

The door is swung open by – Sukie, Jamie's ex. She looks out into the hall at:

Flint and Arliss. Arliss draws breath to speak as Sukie, seeing only two strange men, starts to swing the door shut, but –

– Flint's toe wedges it. He pushes into the apartment, Arliss trailing him, Sukie retreating.

ARLISS

Susanne Shinkleman?

SUKIE

Who the fuck are you?

Flint is pained:

FLINT

Since when do women *curse* like that?

Sukie's hand has groped off as she backs away and it now rises into frame with a canister to –

– pepper-spray Flint.

He screams and covers his eyes with both hands.

Sukie drops the canister and curls a fist.

SUKIE

New millenium, jerk-off.

She punches Flint's unprotected nose. More screams. Alice, the schnauzer, leaps up and down, yapping.

ARLISS

You know Jamie Dobbs?

Sukie kicks Flint in the groin. The screaming stops. Alice's yapping continues.

Agonized, in-drawn breath. Flint sinks to his knees, gasping.

SUKIE

I should've known it was about that cunt!

ARLISS

And Marian Pahlavi? There's no need for that.

Flint, on his knees, blindly gropes under his blazer and brings out a telescoping billy club. He wrist-flips it to full length, his other hand covering his eyes as he croaks:

FLINT

You . . . guttersnipe!

Sukie grabs the end of the club and with a pivot sweeps it around to grab it two-handed from behind Flint. She starts choking him with the club. Arliss doesn't think it's right:

ARLISS

You shouldn't do that, he can't fight back. He can't hit a girl, he's old-school.

FLINT

(*purpling*)

Blrr-gllph . . .

ARLISS

We just want to locate your friends, they inadvertently took something that belongs to us. We don't want to hurt them.

Sukie's words come out with effort as she continues to club-choke Flint:

SUKIE

They're not my *friends*! Hurt 'em as much as you want!

ARLISS

Okay . . . It would be helpful if . . .

FLINT

Glrg . . . rngggluh . . .

ARLISS

. . . if you had a picture?

FLINT

Ga-bluh!

Sukie releases Flint, who collapses from his knees to all fours. The excitable Alice mounts him and humps him.

SUKIE

I got a picture of *one* of them.

Sukie pops a picture out of its tabletop frame: her and Jamie smiling, arm in arm. She rips it in half.

She scribbles something on Jamie's half.

. . . If you find 'em, give it to her.

Arliss takes the picture and looks at it.

ARLISS

Okay. Sure will.

Written on the picture: LOVE WILL BITE YOUR ASS.

THE FINISHED BASEMENT

Linda Ronstadt sings; Marian and Jamie kiss.

Marian breaks away.

MARIAN

I . . .

She stands.

Jamie stares. Both are breathing heavily.

Marian blurts:

. . . If you bring someone back, just . . . I'll take my book to the office . . .

She fights back tears.

. . . I still have a couple of chapters left!

She spins away to the stairs. The other girls make out, unheeding.

JAMIE

Marian!

EARTHQUAKE TRANSITION TO:

CHIEF

Still at Curlie's Drive-Away. We are behind him, close, featuring the phone handset that he holds tensely to his ear.

CHIEF

. . . No, sir. We don't yet know where they are. But we do know exactly *who* they are, we have a picture of one of them, we are all set to –

He listens at the phone. We slowly arc around him as he listens. The arc-around brings Arliss into frame in the background, seated elbows-on-knees, watching the Chief, trying to get a sense of the conversation. The continuing move eventually slips him out of frame.

. . . We will find and deliver the package. Under control . . . Of course you're unhappy, sir; I underst—

The arc-around brings Flint into frame, also sitting waiting. His nose is splinted and his eyes are red and runny.

. . . Yes, I'm putting my two best m—

Click.

The Chief sighs and turns to the two men as he cradles the phone.

. . . All right, get some coffee. You two are going to be driving all night.

GO-GIRL TRANSITION TO:

MARIAN

We are pulling her down a post-war suburban tract street, the kind of neighborhood that would be outside the paneled basement. She's not aware that a car cruises behind her, slowly keeping pace.

After a few beats, a hard spotlight from the car hits her and there's the brief WHOOP *of a siren.*

Marian stops and turns into hard frontlight.

The car also stops but continues to idle. At length a policeman emerges and walks toward her. We hear the crackle of police radio.

Backlit, the cop is only a voice and a shape:

COP

Where you headed, miss?

MARIAN

Home.

COP

And where's that?

Marian has recovered her composure since leaving the party. She's curt, even haughty:

MARIAN

Some motel. I don't know.

COP

You don't know.

MARIAN

I can't remember the *name*. A motel. On the highway.

COP

. . . And where you coming from?

MARIAN

A *house*.

COP

Whose house?

MARIAN

I *don't know*. It was a slumber party.

COP

Little old for slumber parties, aren't you, miss?

Marian draws herself up to full imperious height:

MARIAN

Look, mister.

GO-GIRL TRANSITION TO:

JAMIE

She's sitting into her car. A soccer girl sits into the passenger seat and slides over, giggling, to kiss Jamie and run a hand up her leg.

Jamie, turning to face her, is troubled. A squad car sweeps by behind Jamie, lightbar flashing. The shapes of a cop driving and of a prisoner in the back seat are visible, but Jamie is looking at her soccer friend, and wrestling with a problem.

After a struggling beat:

JAMIE

You know what . . . I'll drop you at home.

SOCCER GIRL

Aww.

RUMBLE-WIPE TO BLACK.

The black is peeled off the opposite way by the countering wipe of a door creaking open. It reveals Jamie, peering into a darkened room.

JAMIE

. . . Marian?

The motel room. Empty. The square-cornered, neatly made bed.

Back to Jamie, disappointed.

MARIAN

Upside down in frame, eyes closed, face striped by the shadows of prison bars. She is asleep on a cot in a lock-up. We're booming down, corkscrewing slowly in.

Ambient noise echoes in the large unseen space outside her cell. Gradually emerging out of the echoes is a rhythmic spring-squeak that loses its reverb as we tighten on Marian.

When we are quite tight on her and our move has put her right-side around, she –

FADES TO BLUE.

The rhythmic spring-squeak carries across the fade.

One squeak is followed, after a short beat, by a young girl rising into frame against a blue now patched by clouds. The girl is an innocent, pigtailed twelve-year-old. A young Marian. She rises in slow motion, reaches her apex, and descends, pigtails lagging.

After she leaves frame, another squeak. She re-enters.

Her point-of-view, booming up: a foreground fence slips down the frame to partly reveal the yard next door. In the yard, a pool. By the pool, a chaise, oriented longways to us, head furthest. On the chaise, a woman. But the apex of our boom is only high enough to bring her into view from the neck up. She lies on her back, sunbathing, eyes covered by a pair of plastic eye-cups linked across the bridge of her nose. We descend.

We intercut with the young girl. Wider shows her in her own backyard, bouncing on a squeaking trampoline.

Succeeding, and higher, bounces bring more of the sunbathing woman into view. She is mature, womanly, attractive. And topless.

The next boom up brings all of the woman into view to reveal that she is not just topless but . . . bottomless. Naked – except for a pair of red-white-and-blue cowboy boots.

PRESENT-DAY MARIAN

In the lock-up. Eyes closed. Dreaming.

The squeaks continue across the cut to –

JAMIE

– who lies in bed in the darkened motel room, hands clasped behind her neck, staring sleeplessly at the ceiling.

The rhythmic squeaks are fainter here, muffled by an intervening wall, and accompanied by the moans of a woman in a neighboring room having sex.

Jamie stares.

PARKING LOT

We're tracking toward the car, parked facing away from us under a mercury vapor light. An ominous drone.

We close in and tip down onto the trunk – LOVE IS A SLEIGH RIDE TO HELL *– and float over it as the drone builds and mixes with:*

Ear-crunching acid rock.

The trunk is now a solid color field filling the frame and the lettering begins to break apart into abstract shapes. The shapes begin to writhe.

Foreground shadows pass across the boiling light-show blobs, which begin to turn into human forms: partygoers, laughing, dancing.

One young woman approaches the camera. She has long dark hair, ironed straight. She smiles sweetly.

YOUNG WOMAN

Hey, handsome . . . Wanna get plastered? . . . get plastered? . . . get plastered? . . .

She and the rest of the image start to fade as does the music, leaving one last echo of the question hanging in . . .

BLACK.

SPINNING GO-GIRL IRIS OUT TO:

AN ORANGE

The abstract spinning, as it slows and stops, resolves into a brightly painted navel orange.

Wider shows the orange to be a cheerful detail in a roadside 'Welcome to Florida!' sign.

A foreground car roars by and takes the image away.

BLACKTOP

We are bird's-eye looking down at an empty frame immediately filled by a speeding-by car. Even though it passes through frame in a flash, the painted slogan on the car's trunk – LOVE IS A SLEIGH RIDE TO HELL – identifies it.

INTERIOR CAR

Jamie is behind the wheel.

After a silent beat of driving:

MARIAN

Thank you.

JAMIE

For what?

MARIAN

Just, picking me up.

JAMIE

Am I not gonna pick you up? Hard not to. 'Ma'am, yer friend is here in the hoosegow, wanna come get her?' I'll come git you all day every day. I will not let a friend of mine rot in prison longer than is absolutely necessary.

MARIAN

And so I say thank you.

JAMIE

I like how you express yourself. Like Jane Eyre. Course, you ain't told me how you come to *be* in prison and I been careful not to ask, but, damn, Marian, *landing* yourself in prison is a very hopeful sign for you.

MARIAN

I think I was in 'jail' not 'prison.'

JAMIE

I am so very sorry, you ain't told me how you come to be in *jail*.

She is looking at Marian who smiles at the implication.

MARIAN

It wasn't hellraising, sorry to disappoint. A policeman didn't like my tone.

JAMIE

Oh, you copped some attitude.

MARIAN

(*with attitude*)

I don't have *attitude*.

JAMIE

Uh-huh. Marian, if I may, there're certain things in life, which you gotta sense, and understand, in order to *live* life, and one of the things you gotta understand is all these funny creatures you probably noticed walkin' around on two legs, we call'm human *beings*? And you gotta understand what makes'm tick, and your whole social situation, you gotta understand what *that* is?

MARIAN

(*not impressed*)

Uh-huh.

JAMIE

You know what that means? 'Social situation'?

MARIAN

I know what 'social situation' means.

JAMIE

Okay, so good, so the whole thing with a cop is, and you should remember this for future reference, that when you're in a social situation with a cop, there *ain't* no social situation.

MARIAN

Uh-huh.

JAMIE

There's a keep-your-fucking-*mouth*-shut situation. There's a 'Yes *sir*' situation is what there is. Believe me, honey-doll, I been dating a cop for two years and I ain't talkin' through m'vulva here.

MARIAN

Thank you, I understand. But if authority is being abused there's an obliga—

JAMIE

Holy shit!

Marian looks at Jamie and follows her look to:

A billboard they approach: 'Re-Elect Gary Channel, U.S. Senate. Faith. Values. Family.' Candidate and family are shown in a heavily retouched color picture: the man stands resting one hand on the shoulder of the blonde wife seated in front of him. On the floor at their feet sit three beautiful blond children. All smile.

Jamie shakes her head.

JAMIE

Florida.

Her head swivels to track the passing billboard. She is somber:

. . . Lesbian, don't let the sun go down on you here.

Bang!

Both girls scream.

Blown tire; Jamie fights to control the wheel.

Skids. Squeals. Screeches and arrhythmic clomps ending in a gravelly schlush *as:*

Exterior: the car is successfully, safely guided onto the shoulder, blown tire clunking into the foreground.

Back to the car interior: A still, silent beat. Both girls finally exhale.

They turn to look at each other, both still wide-eyed.

Simultaneous:

JAMIE AND MARIAN

Y'okay?

ARLISS AND FLINT

Also in a car, Flint driving. Both men, haggard and sleep-deprived, hold styrofoam coffee cups. Flint, squinting against the hard sunlight with satchel-eyes framed by his splinted nose, is especially gruesome.

ARLISS

I'll drive when it's my turn. At the end of three hours. I have no sympathy for you, my friend. You could've just asked her and you'd be fine right now. *I* just asked, she answered. But you cannot relate to the public – which, in a service profession, is a big fucking handicap. And that *hnnkh*-sound is beginning to get irritating.

FLINT

Well, your *lectures* are getting irritating.

ARLISS

I don't lecture, my friend, that's my point. I take people in, I react. I *read* people to get what *I* want. *You*, though, you think life is this orderly series of people to beat the shit out of. Well, real life is not like that. You only see it that way because you're not nourished by human contact, the human give-and-take, so forth. Huh-uh; 'Me want, me take' – that's what *you're* comfortable with.

FLINT

Yeah yeah.

ARLISS

Caveman shit. You don't engage the *whole* person.

FLINT

Well you did a great job helping me engage that . . . harpy.

ARLISS

(*smug*)

Didn't have to. No need whatsoever for the physical approach. Which you couldn't see because you don't savor the stuff of life.

A cellphone chirps.

FLINT

I'm not a sissy-boy, if that's what you mean.

Arliss takes out his phone.

ARLISS

Kiss my ass. Hello?

CHIEF'S VOICE

Okay, we're on track. This girl Marian Pahlavi was picked up for vagrancy last night in Marietta, Georgia. Just north of the Florida border.

BLACK.

At the cut a horizontal slice of picture splits the black and sweeps up: we're looking at Marian and Jamie from inside the trunk.

We cut around as they finish swinging the trunk open. Jamie pulls up the fiberboard panel that covers the spare.

JAMIE

What . . .

There is indeed a tire there, but also a black attaché case.

MARIAN

Something burning?

Steam wisps out from under the attaché case. Marian moves it aside.

Underneath is a hatbox from which the steam wafts up. Cautiously, Marian touches it.

. . . Jamie – it's *cold.*

The two women stare, given pause.

Cars roar by.

A long beat. Marian and Jamie look at each other.

MARIAN

Well, let's see.

She reaches for it. Jamie nervously restrains her.

JAMIE

Maybe we shouldn't. I saw this movie once, where they come across this box, the people in the movie? And they *opened* the box, and it was, like – really bad . . .

Marian's look holds on Jamie as her speech dribbles away. Silence.

Marian turns back and slowly undoes the leather straps that secure the hatbox, which is covered in worn snakeskin. In its day, a fine piece of luggage.

While Marian works, Jamie looks worriedly at the passing cars, as if an outraged motorist might pull over to upbraid them for their nosiness.

The two leather straps are finally undone.

Marian wigglingly works the top off the box. As it comes free, wisps of steam curl up in its draft.

The women look . . .

The women squint . . .

Their eyes widen –

JAMIE

HEAD!

Yes: a human head. Alejandro Santos's, in fact.

Within a swirling vapor of dry ice, his head is drained of color but his thin mustache is still neat. His eyes are rolled up under his tinted glasses and his mouth is agape but, in spite of that, and in spite of the shocked expression he wears, he still looks like a class act.

Jamie screams, and screams, and screams some more.

EARTHQUAKE TRANSITION TO:

LAUGHING

Laughing soccer girls.

The girls are in their pajamas, lounging, in the finished basement, around Arliss and Flint. Arliss smiles; Flint looks darkly out from either side of his nose splint.

ARLISS

No, I'm kidding. It was a minor traffic accident – fast stop, his, uh, face hit the wheel. Looking at a pretty girl, weren't you, Flint?

Arliss winks at the girls and then smiles at Flint.

. . . No more looking at pretty girls for you, right?

Hoarsely, through grit teeth:

FLINT

That's right.

SOCCER GIRL

So are they, like, wanted or something?

ARLISS

(*ever genial*)

Oh, no! No, they aren't in trouble, they just drove off with something we need, didn't even know they had it. So . . . what were you all doing here last night?

SOCCER GIRL 2

Just making out.

ARLISS

Oh yeah? With who?

Laughter from the girls at first takes Arliss by surprise; then he knowingly joins in.

. . . No kiss-and-tell, huh? Heh-heh. Anyway, we need to find those girls to get our . . . sample case back. And when we heard Doreen here paid Marian's fine, we thought, well, you girls might know where they're headed.

SOCCER GIRL 2

How did you know about its being Doreen's check?

FLINT

(*loudly*)

We have contacts in law enforcement.

This dark pronouncement quiets the room.

The girls stare at the glowering man.

GO-GIRL TRANSITION TO:

TRUCKSTOP DINER

Marian and Jamie sit in a booth at the corner, away from the few other diners in the restaurant. They sit together on one side of the table.

The hatbox is not in evidence, but the black attaché case that was also in the trunk rests – closed – on the table in front of them.

JAMIE

No! No! We should just call the cops!

Marian is soothing:

MARIAN

We will, Jamie, but first we should see what's in here.

JAMIE

Why! I don't wanna look! Why do we have to look!

MARIAN

Jamie. Listen. Whoever sliced that head off knows who we are. This might tell us who *they* are, so we won't be at a disadvantage.

JAMIE

The police can find out who they are! And the police can protect us!

MARIAN

Protect us?! They're not the Secret Service! And we're not Chelsea Clinton! What do we lose by looking?

Jamie gives worried thought. Marian presses:

. . . Look. I just want to know what's going on.

She nods at the case.

. . . This might tell us.

JAMIE

I bet it's locked!

By way of answer, Marian reaches with one hand, and – we hear the spring release of one clasp.

A beat.

Jamie slowly reaches. She pops the other clasp.

The women look at each other. A nod from Marian. They hold hands. With their free hands they start to ease the case open.

We slowly close on the two women as the top of the case rises into frame.

Marian's face clouds in dismay and finally curdles in horror. At the same time, Jamie's apprehensive look melts into a great spreading grin.

OUTSIDE

The diner door bangs open and Marian stalks out.

MARIAN

We gotta call the cops!

The attaché case is clamped under her arm; Jamie hurries behind, now unfazed, even chipper.

JAMIE

Why?

MARIAN

That was *awful*!

JAMIE

You just said *not* to call the cops!

MARIAN

In *ignorance*!

JAMIE

No no, what you said was true, and – the cops could think we're involved. You just spent the night in jail.

MARIAN

For *vagrancy*! We wouldn't have anything to do with – *that*!

JAMIE

Okay, cool yer jets, honey, here's what we do.

They have reached their car and now get in.

. . . First: we get to Tallahassee.

SOCCER GIRLS

Crowded at a front door, giggling and waving.

GIRLS

Goodbye!

The reverse shows Flint and Arliss backing down the front walk, headed for their car. Arliss waves back.

ARLISS

Bye, girls! Thanks!

They turn away and Arliss's broad smile quickly drops.

. . . How about next time I do *all* the talking.

FLINT

Sure – gassing is what you're good at.

ARLISS

Well it sure as hell isn't what *you're* good at.

FLINT

I'm not a *suck-up*. Or a *salesman*.

ARLISS

Uh-huh. Would *you* have gotten us the address where they're headed?

He shakes a piece of paper.

. . . I don't think so, Mister Sunshine. Okay . . .

He rounds the car and opens his door.

. . . We've got some hard driving to do.

HOTEL LOBBY

Our two women approach the registration desk. Marian holds the vapor-wisping hatbox, Jamie the attaché case.

CLERK

Welcome to El Conquistador!

JAMIE

Yeah, hiya – you have a room for two, right away?

CLERK

We have something available, yes. How many nights?

Jamie fishes a card from her wallet.

JAMIE

Well, tonight, and then we'll play it by ear. You take the Rainbow Card?

CLERK

Uh . . .

He takes it and examines it.

. . . Oh sure, this is just a, uh, Visa specialty card.

JAMIE

Yeah, but they give a percentage of each purchase to gay-lesbian-bi-transgendered charities. You do that, right?

CLERK

Well, the card issuer would be the –

Marian plops the steaming hatbox onto the desk.

MARIAN

Do you have a super-reinforced safe for sensitive materials?

CLERK

Uh, we have in-room safes for any valuables you –

JAMIE

This place is lesbian-friendly, right?

CLERK

Uh, yes, well, sure, we're friendly to everyone –

MARIAN

Do you have ice?

COUNTRY LANE

It is dusk. Arliss and Flint emerge from their car, bleary-eyed. We hear bones crack as Arliss stretches.

Other cars are scattered on the patch of chewed-up grass that serves as parking lot for the one building within eyeshot: a shack set back from the road. It pulses with amplified blues music.

Arliss and Flint look around.

FLINT

This is it?

Arliss nods at the road.

ARLISS

They said, Farm Road 80. What's the matter? Afraid of the stuff of life?

INSIDE THE SHACK

The walls are painted – though not recently – stark red. Lighting comes from bare bulbs overhead. Cheap Formica tables and chairs are scattered about. The floor is linoleum; one slightly raised section is a bandstand on which a bare-bones blues band performs.

Arliss and Flint look around. They are the only white people and, as such, receive looks. One old man at a table, nodding in time to the music, seems approachable.

Arliss speaks up over the music:

ARLISS

Is this . . . Slappy's?

OLD MAN

Assa.

The old man wears a pork-pie hat and a plaid shirt buttoned to the neck. He has finely wrinkled skin and three teeth that we can see; maybe more, somewhere.

Arliss hands him the picture of Jamie.

ARLISS

Have you seen two, um, non-local, women, come in here? This is one of them.

The old man considers.

OLD MAN

Ise sittin' air lissen June Kimbow cup yees backen *wun* goil cmin peer t'me t'be *half*-local bud eye dough rickalick *two* k'mim ann time *recent*.

Arliss and Flint stare at him. Arliss blinks. Flint continues to stare at the man but speaks to Arliss:

FLINT

What the *fuck* did he just say.

If the old man heard, he is unoffended. Something in the picture interests him. After examining it he hands it back, nodding.

OLD MAN

Ass vair true. Love *wee*-o by cho ass.

SMALL SAFE

At the cut, the open hatbox is placed inside, and then a large chattering baggie full of ice is plopped into the box, on top of the head.

MARIAN

(*off*)

But how do you know they'll be there?

Wider on the room as Jamie closes the safe.

JAMIE

Wait – 6-28-69.

MARIAN

The combination?

JAMIE

Yeah.

MARIAN

. . . Stonewall?

JAMIE

Fuckin' A.

MARIAN

Why send Susanne? They'll just be waiting there, at the drive-away office?

Jamie indicates the attaché case.

JAMIE

Well look at what's in that thing!

Marian doesn't get it.

MARIAN

. . . Yeah?

JAMIE

Well – clearly, this was not a garden-variety decapitation! This is some kind of . . . well, I don't know *what* it is – but they know we have their stuff!

MARIAN

. . . Yeah?

JAMIE

Marian: they can't find *us*, maybe they're waitin' for us to find *them*. That's the only place we'd know to call.

MARIAN

And – why would we get in touch with them?

JAMIE

Sell it back. Shake 'em down. Which, incidentally, is not such a bad idea.

MARIAN

Jamie!

JAMIE

Look. I didn't *invent* extortion.

MARIAN

But, Jamie, why would *Susanne* help us? She *hates* you!

JAMIE

Oh, she's had two days to cool off.

EARTHQUAKE TRANSITION TO:

LOCK-UP

We are in a busy, cluttered precinct house. We are over the shoulder of a female uniformed cop seated at her desk, facing a beefy street thug who has paused, facing out, at the open door of a cell.

COP

Get the fuck back in that lock-up!

THUG

Officer Kracik said I could talk to my attorney –

COP

'Attorney'?! Are you a *college* boy?

His eyes are on her, fearfully.

THUG

. . . Officer Kracik said I could talk to my lawyer.

COP

Officer Kracick ain't running booking! *I'm* running booking! Jackass!

THUG

He said –

COP

You want me to walk over there and kick your street-mugging ass right into the DELAWARE FUCKING RIVER?

(*half-rises from her chair*)

WHO'S RUNNING BOOKING!

The thug backs into the cell.

THUG

You are.

COP

WHO IS?

THUG

You are.

He's closing the door, locking himself in.

COP

No FUCKIN' shit.

VOICE

Shink!

The cop turns to face the camera. It is Sukie.

SUKIE

Yeah.

VOICE

Telephone.

Sukie eases back into her chair and picks up the phone.

SUKIE

Sergeant Shinkleman.

We intercut Jamie, who stands in a phone alcove in the hotel lobby.

JAMIE

Hey. It's me.

SUKIE

Oh. What a lovely surprise.

JAMIE

Sukie, c'mon, let's be friends. I –

SUKIE

Did the two creeps find you?

JAMIE

Two creeps? Whuh, who were they?

SUKIE

(*innocent*)

How would I know? Bill collectors? Herpes patients? Two more people you fucked over, somehow. George and Lennie?

JAMIE

George and Lennie?

SUKIE

Of Mice and Men? Have you read *any books*?

JAMIE

I don't know about that, sugar-plum, but I'm gonna help you break a big murder case.

Sukie nods, skeptically echoing:

SUKIE

You're gonna help me 'break a big murder case' . . . Uh-huh . . . 'Curlie's Drive-Away' . . . Whoa whoa whoa: ask him about the *what* in the attaché case? . . . Jamie, that is about the dumbest thing I've ever heard – and I'm a *cop*.

Back to Jamie:

JAMIE

Why would I make it up? Just go to Curlie's Drive-Away, I guarantee you someone's there . . .

Marian approaches from the elevators. Jamie distractedly holds up a finger: one second.

. . . Fine, if no one's there, you know what? I'll take Alice . . . I swear, yes, pussy-promise. I'll take the dog, you'll never have to deal with her again.

THE CHIEF

He is indeed still at Curlie's. He's on the phone.

CHIEF

Uh-huh . . . Uh-huh . . . *Where* are you?

INTERCUT ARLISS AND FLINT

Arliss talks on his phone as he drives through the country night. Flint, next to him, has a map spread out on his lap.

ARLISS

Wautumpka, Alabama. Well – *outside* of Wautumpka. They hadn't been there, but a very personable music lover told us there's another juke joint, fairly close by, called Champ's – at least I think that's what he said. Maybe he said 'Chance.' Or 'Giants.' Or – 'I ain't certain;' maybe he said 'Ain't-cert' when I asked him the name of the place, but – whatever, I think the soccer team was just confused about which 'joint' these girls were going to, so we're gonna drive –

CHIEF

Stop. Saying. Words. One of the girls finally used a credit card. They arrived in Tallahassee, checked into a hotel called El Conquistador.

Arliss rides for a beat of silence, digesting. Finally:

ARLISS

. . . *Tallahassee.*

CHIEF

I want you to get your asses over there and take care of this, right away.

Beat.

. . . Hello?

ARLISS

. . . *Not* a juke joint.

CHIEF

You should be able to get there by early morning. I'll meet you there.

ARLISS

Uh. I'll level with you, Chief, Flint and me could use a little shut-eye. We haven't slept since the night before last, and we –

He listens at the phone, through which we hear yelling. At length, he reacts to a click.

Chewed out and hung up on, he sadly folds his phone. He stares out at the road, hollow-eyed.

Flint still has his nose in the map.

FLINT

. . . *Who's* in Tallahassee?

FRONT DESK

The desk clerk is again helping Marian and Jamie.

CLERK

Certainly! There are a number of places I could recommend locally or, right here at the hotel we have Espadrilles, which is casual dining, or Baxter's by the Pool, our elegant restaurant down at the lower pool.

JAMIE

(*to Marian*)

Maybe we should stay close.

Marian nods agreement:

MARIAN

(*lowered voice*)

Replenish the ice.

GLITTERING WATER

A leather-bound menu enters frame big, and then there's a cut wide:

The girls are sitting in at an al fresco poolside table as a host hands them menus. The linen and fine silver, the Malibu-lit palm trees with crowns swaying in the ocean breeze, the small jazz combo playing romantic music – the elegance just won't quit.

HOST

Enjoy your meal.

He withdraws.

MARIAN

This is great. But how –

She cuts herself off, apparently because of an arriving waiter.

WAITER

Ladies. Are we starting with drinks?

Marian uses her menu to shield from the waiter a sign to Jamie: a question consisting of the money sign, rubbing thumb against fingers.

Jamie uses her menu to hide her answer back: one hand tracing large arc as she mouths the word 'rainbow.'

Then, aloud, to the waiter:

JAMIE

Champagne, please? Like, a really really good one?

WAITER

Of course.

He withdraws, but Marian keeps her voice lowered:

MARIAN

Won't you have to *pay* for the card? At some point?

Jamie does not show great concern:

JAMIE

Theoretically.

She looks speculatively at Marian, reaches out to take her hand.

. . . So, I've been thinking about this, and it finally dawned on me that you're not the kind of person a girl takes to a roadside motel for a quickie. I mean, I have *heard* of the more soulful sex where you have a nice dinner and conversation first so it all comes out of something deeper, but . . .

(*shrug*)

I usually have stuff to do.

WAITER

The Veuve Clicquot Ponsardin '95.

He pours for Jamie.

Marian so far forgets herself that now she doesn't wait for the waiter to leave. Her voice is unsteady:

MARIAN

You mean – you want to sleep with me?

The waiter waits for the bubbles to subside, then starts topping off Jamie's glass.

JAMIE

Marian, you have got to have a good steamy fuck. It's something I decided last night while I was lying in bed. Before I started masturbating. And I figure, well, if it's important to me, I should take care of it myself. Especially because with you it's got to be with someone who cares for you, am I right? It can't just be a finger jiggling your clit 'n' adiós . . . Thank you.

The waiter has finished Jamie's pour.

WAITER

My pleasure. Madam?

This to Marian, who distractedly accepts.

MARIAN

Yes please. But – is it a good idea for us to have sex? I mean, we're good friends; maybe it's not supposed to be more than that. And maybe we shouldn't risk ruining it.

JAMIE

Well look, you can always figure out reasons not to have sex. And if you think about them too much, guess what.

MARIAN

You never have sex.

JAMIE

Right. Like, my high-school guidance counselor, she was always telling me that this or that would be 'inappropriate.'

MARIAN

Uh-huh.

JAMIE

But once I got her to relax, the sex was great.

WAITER

Ladies, any thoughts about food?

JAMIE

Hang on there, bubba.

She rises and extends a hand to Marian.

. . . First we're gonna dance.

DANCE FLOOR

The women slow-dance, oblivious to the looks they get from the rest of a clientele that is older, conservative. Jamie gazes into Marian's eyes, then leans in to kiss her. After a long kiss they separate and resume gazing at each other.

MARIAN

Maybe I do . . . overthink things.

JAMIE

Yeah, you gotta keep that brain *loose*, honey-darlin', let that mind fly. There was this one time I was with Debbie Augenblick and you know Debbie, she has this humongous dildo she's got mounted on a Black and Decker circular sander, and she had me going like my brains were gonna come out of the top of my friggin' skull, I mean, I came like the Grand Burlington motherfuckin' rail—

Marian grabs Jamie's head with both hands and kisses her, at length and with passion.

A late-middle-aged couple at one table. The man – country-club attire, white mustache, dignified eyebrows – goggles at the two women on the dance floor. His wife gives a stern 'Ahem' to retrieve his attention.

CAR

Arliss and Flint look like hell. Arliss barks with a voice gone hoarse and raised either out of anger or to compete with the wind whipping into his open window:

ARLISS

One accomplishment! Huh? Name me *one*! At least *I'm* in the arena. *Dealing* with people.

FLINT

(*smug*)

Those girls wound you up like a top.

ARLISS

Flint, have you ever fucked a woman. On a creaky porch swing. On a warm summer evening. Crickets? So forth? I mean just fucked her like there's no tomorrow, trousers around your ankles, belt jangling, yelling to beat the band, slammin' away like a Cincinatti jackhammer? *Yes*, people might stroll by and see you looking foolish up there slappin' ham on the veranda. But that is the price you pay for *interaction* – fucking and so forth, blowjobs, jism, whatever – and if this is too *messy* for you, then you will spend the rest of your miserable fucking life just HITTING people and then PULLING your MEASLY little PUD!

FLINT

Can't wait to tell the Chief.

ARLISS

Yeah and why don't you also tell him you're a social fucking IMBECILE that I've been carrying on my BACK all the way from PHILADELPHIA –

FLARING LIGHT

The light travels across the lens. Once it's off the lens and its flare gone we can see Sukie, hand cupped against plate glass, peering from the outside into the darkened interior over which her flashlight continues to play. Her breath rhythmically fogs the glass. As she starts to pan the flashlight the other way, we cut down to:

A point-of-view, up from the floor, of the beam slowly sweeping the wall.

We cut around onto Curlie, who lies on his back, behind the counter, beaten, and bruised, watching the traveling beam. An inarticulate moan.

He weakly slides one hand under some of the loose papers on the floor, product of the office-trashing that went with his beating. As the beam approaches, he summons woozy effort and scoops the papers upward, hoping they'll clear the countertop.

They do – just after the beam passes.

On Sukie outside, finishing the pan of her flashlight and turning away from the window, scowling.

SUKIE

'Big case.'

In the office behind her, in silvery nightlight, we see the lofted papers reach their peak and start to waft down.

We match inside onto Curlie as the papers wig-wag down around him. He croaks through cracked lips:

CURLIE

Won't anybody save Curlie.

Wide outside as Sukie walks – the leather of her utility belt creaking, its cop paraphernalia jingling – to her squad car, which idles in front of Curlie's Drive-Away.

SUKIE

(*grimly*)

. . . That *woman.*

HOTEL ROOM

A hand enters to deposit a long-stemmed champagne glass, half full, on a nightstand.

We pull to the foreground where Marian's head enters frame to drop back against a pillow. She looks dreamily up.

MARIAN

Too much champagne . . .

The body at the nightstand – Jamie's – turns and moves toward us, and her head enters and drops slowly to meet Marian's. The two kiss. As they do so, Jamie nudges the dress straps off of Marian's shoulders.

Jamie rises out of frame, Marian's eyes following.

Marian's dress begins to slide down her body, tugged along by –

Jamie, her hands curled around the hem of the dress, easing it off.

Marian gazes at Jamie, who drops Marian's dress to the floor.

Jamie, uncharacteristically silent, and watching Marian as Marian watches her, begins to undress.

Marian's hand lightly touches her own chest.

. . . pretty . . .

Her fingers trace slow circles on her chest, then slide down out of frame.

Jamie stands watching Marian. At length she climbs onto the bed and lowers herself to kiss Marian. A long kiss during which Marian's arm rhythmically moves.

Jamie draws Marian's hand up between them and they kiss it.

They separate and Jamie slides down Marian's body. On Marian as she arches her back to help Jamie, who from Marian's body-

action must be slipping off her panties. Jamie lingers below frame.

Long hold on Marian. She comes.

Jamie slides back up her body and kisses her, eager for more.

Marian is dreamy. She smiles and murmurs:

> . . . Nice . . .

Jamie's brushing of her lips against Marian's slows, and then stops as she realizes . . .

. . . Marian is asleep. A dainty snore.

Jamie sags. She stares at Marian for a beat, then gives her a kiss on the forehead.

FADE OUT.

Squeaking shocks mix up in the black.

THE CHIEF

Night-driving, as a passenger in a limo. Car steady joins the squeaking shocks that have carried across the cut.

The Chief is reading The Golden Bowl. *After a beat he marks his place with a ribbon, closes the book, then wedges a pillow into the corner formed by seatback and door. He turns off the reading light and closes his eyes.*

CHIEF

> Wake me in Tallahassee.

CHAUFFEUR'S VOICE

> Yes, sir.

A long beat.

FADE OUT.

The squeak carries into the black as the other effects fall away.

FADE UP.

We're framed up square on a fence picket. The squeaking carries across the fade and is now joined by an echoing splish-splash.

A drill bit breaks through the wooden picket – a hand-cranked drill, rotating slowly. It stops, and so does the rhythmic squeak.

The squeak resumes as the drill is cranked the opposite way and withdrawn, leaving a hole.

An eye appears at the hole: young Marian's.

Her point-of-view, vignetted by the hole: the chaise longue next door. It is now empty. A shift in angle through the hole: the cowboy boots have been neatly placed at the lip of the pool. The beautiful neighbor is in the pool doing a lazy backstroke. The water effects have faraway reverb. The squeaking resumes now, different somehow.

DISSOLVE:

Close on adult Marian on her back in bed, its springs squeaking. Her sleeping reverie seems to be moving her to gentle self-stimulation.

LINGERING DISSOLVES:

More on the beautiful neighbor swimming, spiraling through the water.

Young Marian, side-angle, peering through the peephole.

Loud squeaks, accelerating.

Adult Marian, head rolling against the pillow, smiling.

Swimming woman, body cutting through glittering water.

The squeaks come faster and louder.

The neighbor's back door opens with an echoing effect and a slovenly man emerges from the house. His gut hangs over gruesome Bermuda shorts, his face is unshaven and his thinning hair is tufted. He holds a can of Schlitz.

The squeaking slows, becoming less avid.

MAN

(*echoing*)

Honey. We eatin' soon?

WOMAN

Okay.

The man scratches his ass, turns, and goes back inside.

The squeaking has all but stopped.

The beautiful neighbor climbs out of the pool in dripping, glittering slow motion.

Young Marian watching.

The squeaking picks up again.

The beautiful neighbor's breasts joggle as she tosses her hair, throwing off sparkling water.

The squeaking is frenzied. In rhythm with the bedsprings, there is moaning.

The beautiful neighbor bends to pick up her cowboy boots.

Rasping breath.

Close on the adult Marian. Dawn in the hotel room. Marian still wears a dreamy smile, but the jiggling of the bed beneath her now seems more vigorous than can be explained by her own body's movement. Nor is the ragged breathing coming from her.

The breath grows shorter and shorter and the moaning louder and louder. The activity slowly rouses Marian: her eyelids flutter open; she begins to focus, and we widen out to discover, as she does:

Jamie lying next to her. The sheet mostly covers her but she has one leg pulled back with one hand and its cowboy-booted foot is pointed up at the ceiling. Beneath the sheet her other hand pumps furiously.

MARIAN
(*groggily*)

. . . Jamie?

Without looking over, between gasps:

JAMIE

Waited . . . for you . . . as long as I . . . oh! . . . OH!

Marian looks over at:

The attaché case, open on the night table.

MARIAN
(*horrified*)

Jamie!

JAMIE

OH! OH!

Marian leaps from the bed.

MARIAN

No, Jamie, *no*!

Marian looks into the open attaché case and we, for the first time, see inside:

It is felt-lined, with molded indentations to keep its contents cushioned and in place. A row of . . . phalluses, not identical, but all erect, some quite impressive.

The leftmost phallus pocket is empty.

Marian stifles a sob.

. . . Why, Jamie, *why*?

JAMIE

OHH, MARIAN!

THE CHIEF

Jiggling.

VOICE

. . . Sir?

Responding to the shaking, the Chief stirs and opens his eyes.

The chauffeur, who was leaning in to shake him, straightens.

. . . Tallahassee, sir. Where to, exactly?

CHIEF

. . . Mm. Uh . . .

He blinks sleep from his eyes, looks groggily about, and then looks at his watch.

. . . Yes. The track.

HOTEL ROOM

Jamie lies back, catching her breath.

JAMIE

. . . Soooo good . . .

A voice from the bathroom:

MARIAN

Why did you *do* that!

Marian appears at the bathroom door, tearfully cinching the belt on a hotel bathrobe. Jamie props herself on her elbows.

JAMIE

Come on, Marian, I thought you were gonna loosen up.

MARIAN

Are you gonna work your way through all of them?!

JAMIE

Nah, I like this one. Aww, don't be mad; last night was beautiful, but you were drunk and I didn't get my turn on the water slide if you know what I mean –

CRASH! The door bangs open.

The women scream.

Arliss and Flint are rumpled and wild-eyed. Arliss barks as Flint agitatedly aims and re-aims a gun held police-style in front of him.

ARLISS

All right! We want the hatbox and the – whoa. She's naked. All right. No big deal! Just a naked lady! We want the hatbox and the – careful with that thing, you fucking moron!

FLINT

Screw you!

ARLISS

All right! We want the – yeah, this!

He slams the attaché case shut and tucks it under his arm.

. . . Please and thank you! And the headbox!

FLINT

*Hat*box!

ARLISS

Fuck you! Don't you fucking lecture me! Clothes on, ladies! Please and thank you! All friends here! ALL right! Let's get this show on the road!

Acid rock – the familiar, Bay Area Summer of Love interminable-guitar-solo rock – comes out of nowhere and slams us into –

BLACK.

After a long beat of black the music rolls across a hard cut to –

– the woman with the ironed hair. Her hands, down out of frame, are doing something that makes a gloopy slurping sound. She looks smilingly into the lens.

WOMAN

Yes, baby . . . You are such a big . . . bouncy . . . beautiful . . . baby . . .

MAN'S VOICE

Whoa . . .

Reverse on the man, lying flat on his back, but rolling his head forward to look down his body. He is college-aged and has long hair kept in place by a beaded Indian headband. He is stoned.

. . . this is so groovy.

WOMAN

Love doesn't have to die, baby . . .

Her hands continue to work, continuing the gloopy slurping.

. . . Now I'll get to love you forever . . . and ever . . .

Something deep builds on the track: rolling thunder? stampeding cattle? rain drumming on a roof?

The man chimes idiotically along with the woman:

MAN AND WOMAN

. . . and ever . . . and ever . . . never to wilt . . . never to wane . . . never to wilt . . . never to wane . . .

The deep drumming builds and propels us into a cut to:

DOGS' FEET

Thundering by. Their yelps bang in with the cut.

BLACK.

The thundering feet and the yipping continue.

The black wipes quickly up and away to a –

WINDOWLESS ROOM

Arliss backs away from the lens, looking down into it in low shot, holding a blindfold. Flint stands just behind him.

The thunder of the dogs, in muffled perspective here, begins to recede.

Arliss's speech echoes in the empty room.

ARLISS

– came straight here. Haven't debriefed 'em, Chief, figured you'd want to do the talking.

Echoing footsteps approach. The Chief enters the bottom of frame from deep and strides into the foreground. His jaw is tight with anger.

CHIEF

That's all they had?

ARLISS

What's all they had?

The Chief glares briefly at Arliss. He looks down into the lens.

CHIEF

Ladies, you're a day late and a dick short.

Reverse finally shows Jamie and Marian. They are gagged and bound into a couple of stadium seats, many of which are stored in this fluorescent-lit room along with other racetrack trappings.

Arliss stares at the Chief.

ARLISS

What are you talking about?

CHIEF

The senator's penis was not in the case!

Arliss is stunned.

ARLISS

Not in the . . .

FLINT

Well that just figures.

CHIEF

Come on, girls! Where's the last phallus?

Marian shakes her head and makes shrugging motions. Jamie, cuing off her, does likewise, projecting wide-eyed ignorance.

CHIEF

(*to Arliss*)

You didn't check the case before you left?

ARLISS

I – I –

FLINT

He's been stepping on his own dick the whole way down, Chief!

ARLISS

FUCK YOU! WHAT HAVE *YOU* DONE, JERK-OFF?

FLINT

I GOT THE SPANISH GUY'S HEAD, EINSTEIN!

ARLISS

THEY *GAVE* YOU THE COMBINATION! AND IT *STILL* TOOK YOU FIFTEEN MINUTES –

FLINT

I HAVEN'T SLEPT SINCE TUESDAY!

ARLISS

– RIGHT, LEFT, *PAST* THE FIRST NUMBER –

GATES

Slapping open. Yelping dogs emerge to start a new race.

HOTEL HALLWAY

The thundering dogs drop out, replaced by sedate muzak.

Far down the hall, a maid slowly pushes her cart toward us.

WINDOWLESS ROOM

The rumble of the approaching dogs.

CHIEF

The senator is a good man. He smoked marijuana once in college . . .

The Chief is looking earnestly into the lens. Seated with an elbow on one knee, leaning in to his audience, he shrugs.

. . . Many of us did. It was a different time . . .

Reverse shows the two women gagged and wide-eyed. They nod understanding.

We can hear, though not see, Arliss and Flint shouting at each other elsewhere in the room. The Chief does his best to ignore it. He gives the girls a smile meant to signify sweet reason and good intentions.

. . . He was at a party . . . He met a girl. A 'hippie chick' . . . Tiffany Plastercaster . . .

DOG'S FEET

Pounding the track in slow motion, scattering divots of earth.

HOTEL HALLWAY

Sweet muzak. The maid with the cart – she is Hispanic and wears a small gold crucifix at her neck – has reached the foreground door. She knocks.

MAID

How ski peen!

No answer. She inserts her passcard in the lock.

DOGS

Thundering into a turn.

THE CHIEF

He leans in closer so that he can keep his voice low and still be heard over the shouting in the background, which is growing more agitated.

CHIEF

... A party girl. She took a plaster cast of his ... his excited ... thing. And poured one ... replica. She made one model of each of her

(*finger-quotes*)

'old men.'

He swallows hard.

He continues:

... The senator didn't know, then, that later in life he'd be called on to serve his community ... his state ... perhaps – some day – his nation ...

He pleads, responding to some unspoken – perhaps inner? – reproach:

... He was just a kid!

He shakes his head, composes himself.

... His penis passed from hand to hand. It finally ended up with an international collector named Alejandro Santos y Obrador. You saw him – sort of.

MOTEL ROOM

Jamie and Marian's room. The maid takes the pillows from the rumpled bed and dumps them onto a chair.

WINDOWLESS ROOM

The dogs are getting closer, pounding, yapping.

We are in a choking close-up of the Chief.

CHIEF

This penis cannot become a piece of merchandise. Think of it [illegible] eBay . . . 'Senator Gary Channel's – wiener! Lightly used!' Comments! Reviews! Think of what it would do to him! His children! His family! His career! We'll *pay* for it! We're not unreasonable! We just – WILL YOU SHUT UP?!

Arliss and Flint's shouting has built to a crescendo. They bellow, off:

FLINT

That wasn't *my* idea!

ARLISS

I was just trying to keep us awake! I was experimenting! But you *liked* it – I could tell!

FLINT

No, I *didn't* – I, it was the Irish coffee, I was drunk, I –

ARLISS

Drunk on *cock*!

FLINT

No, I –

ARLISS

It's not *my* thing! I was just trying to help you be a man! To understand life!

FLINT

NO –

ARLISS

The stuff of life!

FLINT

NO! NO! NO!

BANG!

Screams.

BANG! BANG!

The Chief is looking off, horrified.

Pounding dog feet.

The two women look at each other.

The Chief leaps to his feet and runs out of frame. Off:

CHIEF

Good god, man! Get a grip on yourself! What in the name of –

BANG! BANG!

Hysterical sobbing.

The women, wide-eyed, crane around as far as their bindings permit.

Their point-of-view, a sloppy pan-around ending in an unbalanced frame: at the far end of the room, composing a shaky tableau, are Arliss's body in a pool of spreading blood, and the Chief's in an ungainly heap.

Flint is agitatedly putting his gun in the Chief's limp hand and clumsily closing the Chief's fingers around it.

Flint looks up at the lens – a deer in the headlights.

He gapes for a moment.

He rips the gun from the dead man's hand and swings it toward us, sobbing.

The girls shriek into their gags as their heads swing forward and they cringe, awaiting the . . .

Click.

They look back around.

The same sloppy pan-around ends with the slop-tilted and off-balance frame of Flint aiming the gun at us.

He vainly squeezes the trigger on two more empty chambers. He chokes out a weak –

FLINT

. . . Mommy!

– and then, sobbing, he turns, flings a door open, and runs.

Marian's hands, bound behind her back, wriggle to get a couple of fingers up to the knot at her wrist.

HOTEL ROOM

Very close on the maid who is on her knees beside the bed, her head just above the mattress as she reaches beneath the covers to tug at the fitted sheet, trying to get it flat. Her gold crucifix sways as she works.

She freezes, coming across something in the sheets. She frowns.

Her eyes drift as she tries to figure out by touch what it is.

She finally withdraws the penis from the bed and holds it before her face. For a long moment she stares in incomprehension, and then . . .

SCREAMS.

DOGS

Compressed by a long lens, charging at us in slow motion, tongues glogging to and fro.

HALLWAY

A wide curving hallway somewhere under the stands. Track patrons mill. At the cut, a door onto the hall bursts open and the two women spill out, Marian holding the hatbox and Jamie the attaché case. After a quick look in both directions:

MARIAN

We have to get back to the hotel and grab the penis out of the bed. Then we switch hotels –

JAMIE

You get the penis; I'll meet you at the new hotel.

MARIAN

Okay. The La Lanterna. I'll check in under the name . . . Abzug. Where you going?

JAMIE

Art store.

GO-GIRL TRANSITION TO:

PET CARRIER

We are close on a pet-carrying case. Annoying yaps come from inside. Above the case's little door is an engraved nameplate: ALICE B. TOKLAS.

Wider shows Sukie, in civilian clothes, holding the case, on line at a ticket counter at the Philadelphia airport. At an agent's prompt of 'Next customer,' Sukie picks up the case and approaches the counter.

SUKIE

Susanne Shinkleman, going to Tallahassee, don't ask me *why*.

TALLAHASSEE LIVING

The glossy magazine, lying on a coffee table, has Gary Channel on its cover. He's in a pastel cashmere sweater, at home, relaxed, or posing as 'relaxed,' beaming at the lens. The tasteful interior reeks of Southern living. His wife, posed with him, displays the same performed warmth.

We hear the beeps of a phone number being dialed and, on connection, a phone-filtered ring. A phone-filtered voice:

VOICE

Committee to Re-Elect.

A shopping bag from Tallahassee Arts & Crafts is plopped down onto the magazine and we jump back:

We're in a new hotel room. Jamie, with the phone handset wedged into her shoulder, has just set down the arts-store bag and she starts pulling supplies from it.

JAMIE

I need to speak to the senator.

VOICE

Well – who is this?

JAMIE

The person who has his . . . personal effects.

A BED

We're wide on the old hotel room's bed, now perfectly made. We hold on it for a still beat.

The reverse shows Marian, frozen at the open door, staring at the bed.

Another beat and she unfreezes, finishes entering, and lets the door swing shut behind her.

BATHROOM

The lights flicker on. Marian, hand at the light switch, looks around. Her look is arrested by:

A row of toiletries at the sink. Shampoo, lotions, shower cap, soaps, an extra roll of toilet paper unwrapped but bound with red ribbon. Also wearing a red ribbon is the senator's penis, in line with the toiletries, propped upright against the backsplash.

An ominous rumble builds on the track.

CARGO HOLD

The rumble bumps up at the cut: airplane steady. Entering at the cut is an annoying yapping sound.

We are in a semi-dark hold, tracking in on a pet carrier surrounded by other luggage jiggling with the motion of the plane. The yapping grows louder as we drift in.

BACK TO THE NEW HOTEL ROOM

Deluxe quiet.

Jamie stands still, listening at the phone.

Finally, the click of a connection and:

NEW VOICE

Who is this.

JAMIE

. . . Senator?

VOICE

Yes. Who is this.

JAMIE

Somebody who wants a million dollars.

No answer.

. . . If you can get it by tonight, you can have your thing back. *Every*body's things.

No answer.

. . . I'll tell you where to bring the money. Come alone. If you're not alone, believe me, I'll know it.

A long beat. Finally:

VOICE

Where do I go.

LOBBY OF OLD HOTEL

Sukie is at the front desk, holding the carrier from which yapping still emanates.

SUKIE

Someone named Jamie Dobbs made a call . . .

She jerks a thumb over her shoulder, indicating the lobby phone.

. . . from that phone. Last night.

The desk clerk nods.

CLERK

Yes, uh-huh.

Sukie hoists the yapping carrier onto the counter.

SUKIE

Well this is for her.

CLERK

Oh, I'm sorry, ma'am, you missed them. Her friend just checked them out.

NEW HOTEL

Marian has settled onto the couch and is just finishing The Europeans. *She thoughtfully closes the book and is setting it aside when Jamie emerges from the bathroom, dusty and disheveled.*

JAMIE

Done.

MARIAN

With what?

JAMIE

Tell you later, I'm gonna clean up. Wanna join me?

RACETRACK INTERROGATION ROOM

The Chief, in the foreground, stares sightlessly into the lens, mouth agape and one cheek squushed against the floor. A soft shape behind him is the dead Arliss.

After a quiet beat we hear the muffled chirping of the Chief's cellphone. It's tucked somewhere in his suit. The ringtone is 'Happy Days Are Here Again.'

The ring stops. The Chief stares on.

At length, a cheerful WHOOP signals that a message has been left.

HOTEL BATHROOM

We're looking at the glass-enclosed shower which is steaming up. Two female shapes are entwined inside.

We cut inside to Marian and Jamie, kissing.

MARIAN

Jamie . . . I . . . I want . . .

JAMIE

Uh-huh?

MARIAN

I . . . I want . . .

Jamie separates and looks at her encouragingly.

JAMIE

What do you want, sugar-sweet?

Marian finds her resolve:

MARIAN

I want to make love with the senator's penis!

The girls stare at each other, Jamie wise, Marian wide-eyed and a little fearful, like the first day at sleepaway camp.

We cut outside the shower as Jamie's hand nudges its door open and gropes. We travel with the hand to bring in a penis standing upright on the counter nearby. The hand blindly bumps it – it tips, wobbles – and then saves it, closes firmly over it, and withdraws it into the shower.

We ease wider to see shapes in the shower, a diffused pantomime of sex, the scene lent misty lyricism by the steam inside. As sound starts to climax we cut to:

A STATUE

Underlit like William Penn, but this gentleman is bearded, helmeted, Spanish: a conquistador. He holds a sword raised at a suggestive angle from his hips.

We cut down to an identifying plaque: Ponce De Leon.

We cut over the shoulder of Ponce de Leon and his sword. A bar sign is visible halfway down this Tallahassee street: THE SHE SHED.

INSIDE THE BAR

We track slowly toward the back of the narrow room, bar on one side and booths on the other. It's the same configuration as the Alejandro Santos bar at the beginning of the movie, and the same shot introducing it, but this establishment is more crowded, and . . .

. . . the clientele is entirely female. Lesbians only, lining the bar and at every table, until we come to . . .

. . . the second booth to last. A man is peeking around from behind his bench back, a Dutch-boy hat drawn down over his eyes to cover as much of his face as possible – but we recognize

Senator Gary Channel from his billboard. We close on him looking apprehensively toward the front of the establishment.

He gives up looking and swings his shoulders back into the booth. He's hugging a brown attaché case to his chest.

JAMIE'S VOICE

We feel as if we know you.

The senator starts.

The girls have approached from the back of the bar. Jamie stands holding the black attaché case, Marian the hatbox.

SENATOR

Who are you?

The two women stare at him, weighing all the possible answers. Finally Marian spits out:

MARIAN

Democrats.

JAMIE

. . . Mind if we sit down?

She's sitting even as she asks. The senator nods at their attaché case.

SENATOR

They all there?

By way of answer – ba-doing – *Jamie pops the clasps on the case, opens it, and pivots it on the tabletop so that the senator may look.*

MARIAN

Count 'em.

The senator stares coldly at the women. At length his eyes shift down to the penises. His look becomes thoughtful.

SENATOR

We didn't deserve this – commodification. These are all good people. Important people, too, some of them . . .

An insert on the row of penises, the set now complete.

. . . There's the head of one of the bigger Fortune 500 companies . . . an owner of a large-market football team . . . a Supreme Court justice.

The senator's look shifts up to the girls and becomes scornful.

. . . And you little people titillate yourselves with something that was never meant for you, trafficking in other people's . . . attainments.

MARIAN

Senator, save the sanctimony.

JAMIE

And hand over the million smackers.

The senator pushes his attaché case across the table.

SENATOR

I used to believe in the unfettered free market.

A sad shake of the head.

. . . I don't know.

He lowers the lid on the penis case, snaps it shut, and rises, grabbing it and the hatbox.

MARIAN

Whose head, Senator?

The Senator looks down at her through narrowed eyes:

SENATOR

Don't get lofty with me. *Women.*

He leaves.

The girls watch him go. Marian's lingering look is haunted.

MARIAN

Did we do the wrong thing?

Jamie looks at her interrogatively. Marian meets her look.

. . . What if he's the next president?

VOICE

You girls are cute.

They look up:

A large motorcycle lesbian.

. . . My friends 'n' me are having a basement party. Wanna join us?

Marian and Jamie look at each other, considering. Something sweet passes between them, and Jamie smiles up at the motorcycle lesbian.

JAMIE

Not tonight.

She and Marian rise, holding hands.

EXTERIOR

We boom down off the bar's sign to meet Marian and Jamie coming out of the bar just as – thoomp – *they run into someone going in. There's loud yapping at the impact.*

JAMIE

Sukie!

A reverse shows that it is indeed her, with the pet carrier.

SUKIE

Here you are. So what was that crackhead phone call about?

JAMIE

What do you mean? How'd you know I'd be here?

SUKIE

How many dyke bars are there in Tallahassee.

Jump back: a long-lens view of the three women in front of the bar among the other lesbians who are out on the sidewalk enjoying the fresh night air. Ponce de Leon is deep behind them, sword upraised.

A reverse shows this to have been the point-of-view of Senator Channel, lurking at the mouth of an alley across the street. He pulls off his Dutch-boy cap and tosses it aside. He pulls on what looks like a black stocking cap and picks up his attaché case and hatbox.

Close again on the women:

SUKIE

Oh, you're an executive now?

She refers to Jamie's attaché case.

. . . Don't tell me: they made you president of Little Miss Liarpants, Inc.

JAMIE

This? No, I just, uh . . .

Intercut: pulling Senator Channel out into the street.

His point-of-view: tracking toward the knot of lesbians in front of the bar, Marian and Jamie with their backs to us.

The statue: Ponce de Leon, sinisterly underlit.

The senator: tucking his attaché case under the arm that holds the hatbox and with his freed hand reaching up to his black stocking cap.

The women:

MARIAN

– we thought they didn't know where we were but somehow they did and this morning they threw us in the back of a Toyota Tercel and took us to the dog track and I'm sure they were gonna kill us but lucky for us they'd left the most important penis behind.

Sukie stares at her, deadpan.

SUKIE

Well. You've had a full day.

She holds the yapping carrier out to Jamie.

. . . She's yours now.

Her attention is caught by something up the street:

Deep behind Marian and Jamie, Senator Channel strides purposefully toward them, rolling a black balaclava down to cover his face.

Sukie sets down the carrier.

. . . Hang on.

Senator Channel is reaching under his coat.

. . . This doesn't look good.

Sukie opens the door to the carrier. She reaches in and, in addition to frantic skittering and yapping inside, we hear the tearing sound of adhesive giving way.

As Sukie straightens, Marian and Jamie turn to look where she's looking.

Senator Channel is leveling a gun.

Screams.

BLAM! BLAM!

Not his gun.

Furious yapping.

The senator pitches back, letting sail the hatbox.

Sukie is holding a smoking police special, duct tape stuck to it.

The hatbox hits the ground behind the senator. Its wet seams give. Ice clatters out with the . . .

. . . head, which rolls away.

Screams from the bystanders.

Senator Channel writhes on the ground.

SENATOR

When did they start . . . arming . . . *lesbians?*

Alejandro Santos's head bumps off down the street with the eccentric action of an irregular spheroid. Alice the schnauzer, snarling and yapping, gives furious chase.

As lesbians scream around them, Sukie, Jamie and Marian watch the receding head.

After a beat, her gaze still distant:

SUKIE

What's she chasing?

Jamie too is gazing down the street.

JAMIE

. . . We forgot to tell you about the suave guy's head in the hatbox . . .

The three women, watching as the trundling head and yapping dog recede.

Ponce de Leon, not reacting.

FADE OUT.

NEWSPAPER

The next day's paper is headlined: SENATOR CHANNEL SHOT OUTSIDE LESBIAN BAR. Subhead: CARRYING HUMAN HEAD, PLASTER PENISES. Sub-subhead: 'I CAN EXPLAIN' SAYS RECOVERING LEGISLATOR.

JAMIE

(*off*)

Boy. I think *I* could win against him.

Wider shows the two women at an umbrella-shaded table by their new hotel's pool. Jamie is looking at the paper as they sip tropical drinks.

. . . And now we get to just keep on going – who's gonna complain if we keep the car? Things could not have worked out better.

MARIAN
(*down*)

Well . . . I guess.

JAMIE

What's wrong?

MARIAN

I . . . am fully aware that this senator is a terrible person. But I have to admit, I'll miss his . . .

JAMIE

Oh, no worries, girl.

She leans down to the Tallahassee Arts & Crafts bag at her feet.

. . . I made a cast . . .

She opens the bag to show Marian.

. . . And two copies.

And indeed, in the bag are two gleaming new penises. Marian brightens.

MARIAN

Great! But – why two?

JAMIE

For each other . . .

BELLBOY

Ladies, your visitor is here.

As Jamie rises:

JAMIE

. . . You know, Hers and Hers?

(*to the bellboy*)

Can we get our car?

FRONT STEPS

The girls emerge. Marian reacts to someone in a big straw sunhat waiting down at the drive, her back to us:

MARIAN

Aunt Ellis!

The woman turns: a bespectacled elderly black lady.

AUNT ELLIS

Hello darlin'.

Jamie reacts. As they descend the steps:

JAMIE

She's your aunt?

MARIAN

Uh-huh, Uncle John met her in church.

They have almost arrived.

(*under her breath*)

Watch what you say – she's very religious.

She hugs her aunt as their car is pulled up.

. . . This is my friend Jamie.

AUNT ELLIS

How're you, young lady? Is this your first time in Tallahassee?

They're getting into the car, Marian behind the wheel, Aunt Ellis in the middle.

JAMIE

Oh yes, ma'am, and what a beautiful city! Not like *Miami*!

AUNT ELLIS

No, noooo – not like *Miami*. You be able to stay with us long?

MARIAN

No, unfortunately –

JAMIE

(*vivacious*)

Right after the birding we're off for Massachusetts. We just decided last night.

MARIAN

(*tensing*)

Jamie –

AUNT ELLIS

Well now what do they have in Massachusetts that we don't have right here in North Florida.

JAMIE

Women can get married there!

Marian goes rigid, closes her eyes.

Aunt Ellis stares at Jamie. A beat.

AUNT ELLIS

What – to each *other*?

Aunt Ellis looks from Jamie, beaming, to her other side where Marian sits stiffly focused forward.

. . . Huh!

Aunt Ellis's look goes forward and she muses as she folds her hands over her enormous old-lady purse.

. . . That's an *innovation*.

As Marian relaxes and puts the car in gear, we cut to the trunk. Jamie's art – LOVE IS A SLEIGH RIDE TO HELL – has been modified. The 't' in 'to' has been overpainted to make it an 's,' and 'hell' has been turned into 'here.' And one word has been added:

LOVE IS A SLEIGH RIDE – SO HERE GOES!

We tip up off the trunk as the car pulls away. As we watch the car recede, the bellboy's back enters. He holds aloft by its tote-string the Tallahassee Arts & Crafts bag and calls toward the departing car:

BELLBOY

Ladies!

But the women don't hear and the car disappears round the bend of the hotel drive.

The bellboy shakes his head, looks down at the bag.

Something snags his look.

A beat.

He grabs the bag by its two sides and, on the crinkle-clunk of him pulling it wider to look inside, we:

CUT TO BLACK

After the end credits, a teaser for the sequel: *Dykes Redux: Here Come the Brides.*

An F&F double: two Fabers,
two authors, two stories – *too much!*

Faber brings you a Honey O'Donahue Mystery
While Faber brings you a sizzling story of love on the run.

Honey Don't! and *Drive-Away Dykes!*

Two covers can barely contain the action!

About the Authors

JUAN CARLOS DAMIGO emigrated to Miami from his native Cuba in 1968, at the tender age of fifteen. Almost immediately Juan developed a love of 1970s variety television and learned to speak English through continuous viewings of the sketch comedy routines of Shields and Yarnell.

During these formative years Juan also developed a love of American literature by way of author Arthur Hailey. After graduating from Arkassippi Polytechnic, Juan published his first novel, *Too Much Love for One Man*, under the pen name Ethan Coen.

A former Kern County sheriff's deputy, and the law enforcement advisor for the hit NBC series *Police Woman*, TRICIA COOKE is also known for her hard-hitting activist journalism for the *LA Alt* and the *San Fernando Expat*. Tricia was the recipient of the 1972 Hal Fishman Award in Journalistic Excellence for her 1971 article, 'Doug Henning: It's not magic . . . it's cocaine.'

After meeting at an international conference on the lesbian antinomies of Immanuel Kant, Cooke and Damigo decided to team up for the first of their three literary collaborations, *Drive-Away Dykes*.

Damigo currently resides in Gorham, New Hampshire, with his four cats and a miniature potbelly pig named Peppers. Cooke resides in Millville, New Jersey.

Compiled by Stefan Dechant

HONEY DON'T!

by the same authors

DRIVE-AWAY DYKES

HONEY DON'T!

The screenplay

ETHAN COEN AND TRICIA COOKE

faber

First published in 2025
by Faber & Faber Ltd
The Bindery, 51 Hatton Garden
London EC1N 8HN

First published in the USA in 2025

Typeset by Brighton Gray
Printed and bound by CPI Group (UK) Ltd, Croydon, CR0 4YY

A CIP record for this book is available from the British Library

ISBN 978–0–571–39912–3

2 4 6 8 10 9 7 5 3 1

HONEY DON'T!

BLUE SKY

We hear desert insects.

Long hold.

Panting nears. And scuffing of feet against rock, getting closer with the panting.

A woman's head rises into frame. She pauses, breathing heavily, in low shot against the blue sky. She's attractive, brunette. She gazes down.

Now she continues forward – descending, revealing that her pause had been at the crest of a hill. She wears tight capri pants and a shirt knotted at the midriff. She's descending a rock scree. Rocks clatter away as she descends. Insects fall to silence, then resume chirring once she's past.

She arrives at the bottom of the ravine where a wrecked car rests on its roof. It has tumbled a long way. Inside the car a woman rests head-bent against the roof, eyes open. She is pretty, and bloody, and still.

The brunette appears beyond her, at her window, and stoops to peer in. She is unperturbed by what she sees.

She picks up the lifeless arm nearest her and looks at the hand. She lets the arm flop back down.

She lies flat on her belly and reaches in across the woman's crumpled body and grabs the far arm. She pulls. Her tugging disarranges the body inside. She finally gets the arm fully across the body, hand extending outside the window.

She straightens the woman's still-flexible fingers. On one finger is a ring whose insignia seems mysteriously – almost

Masonically – meaningful: four faceted triangles pointing out from a central hub, like a compass key on an old map.

The brunette tugs at the ring. It's tight. She pulls harder. Finger-skin bunches.

Grimacing, she twists and tugs with a purpose. We hear the dead body inside the car shifting with the tug's force.

The ring comes off and the freed hand flops to the ground. The brunette stands.

She slips the ring into the tight front pocket of her capri pants.

CANYON RIVER

The brunette, sweaty and dusty from her mission in the nearby ravine, strips and leaves her clothes on the shore.

She swims, taking physical pleasure in it, luxuriating in water against flesh.

She emerges from the water and wraps her shirt turban-like around her wet hair. She puts on leopard-print panties and bra.

She carries the rest of her clothes to a scooter parked roadside. Its leopard-print trim matches her underwear.

From her pants pocket she pulls the mysterious ring and some keys. She puts the signet ring back in the pants and stows the pants in the scooter's bin. She unwraps her hair and stows her shirt. She climbs onto the scooter, keys the ignition, and roars off.

She rides the winding canyon road in her undies, enjoying the sun on her face and the wind in her hair.

BLACK.

HEAD CREDITS.

Music plays over a scene-setting Southern California montage. Not prosperous Southern California but cities like Lancaster, Palmdale, Bakersfield – places baked, blasted, and bleak. Houses sit on dusty lots behind chain-link fences, front windows papered over, front yards holding car skeletons not swing sets, signs that say NO TRESPASSING, *or personalized variants like* I GOT A DOG AND A SHOTGUN AND I DON'T LIKE VISITORS.

And city scenes: folk-art murals on beige brick walls in slanting sun, cracked sidewalks, shuttered storefronts, billboards for personal injury lawyers.

And sprinkled throughout are shots of that icon of the underclass: the bus.

The bus making its cumbersome way through the city. Its roof pipe adding rippling exhaust to the heat of the streets. The pleats of its chassis-extender. A graffitied ad on its side.

A route map on a post, marking a stop. Gutter, curb, an awning over a hard plastic bench. The bus trundles in. Its door hisses hydraulically down. Nobody running to catch it; you wait for the bus. Many bus stops, and people waiting, staring, waiting.

A junkie nodding off at a bus stop. Another bus stop: a squad car trolls by. The officers' traveling point-of-view: a young woman at the stop, ratty backpack, ripped jeans, greasy hair – a runaway, or homeless, or the bus is the way home and it's a long way home.

Music and credits end on a cut to an apartment interior: close on a window-mounted air conditioner working mightily. The window has white louvers closed against hard sun.

We pan the apartment, crossing a couple of glasses resting on a coffee table, red wine puddled at the bottom of each, lipstick smudging the rim of one.

The pan leaves the glasses, and the table, and tips down to the floor where a dress lies discarded. The foot of a bed comes into

frame. We travel up the bed to bring in one of its occupants: a young woman, lanky and androgynous. Her hair is mussed, her face lightly flushed, she smiles dreamily in her sleep.

A ringtone.

We hear the far occupant of the bed – hidden by the foreground woman – groping for the phone. The phone is thumbed on and Honey reveals herself, rising to prop herself on one elbow. She's an attractive woman a little older than her bedmate. She gives a bleary:

HONEY

Hello . . . Where? . . . Okay . . . Yeah, okay.

She hangs up.

She swings her feet off the bed and, sitting back to us, looks down at the floor in front of her. She leans and picks up a bra and puts it on. As the woman next to her stirs, she leans again for panties and pulls them on.

The woman looks around, getting her bearings. As the cobwebs clear she gazes at Honey and smiles.

YOUNG WOMAN

That was amazing.

HONEY

Yeah it was. Gotta go out. Door'll lock behind you.

CRASH SCENE

Honey is picking her way down into the ravine now crowded with police and fire-department personnel.

VOICE

Honey O'Donahue!

It is Marty Metakawitch, a plain-clothes detective sipping coffee from a cardboard cup.

. . . Twutta we owe the onna? This girl a client? Medical examiner's on his way out, gonna render an opinion is she dead or not. Whatta you think?

Honey has made her way down to Marty who stands over the woman's body which has been extricated from the car. The woman lies on the ground staring sightlessly up, dried blood on her face.

Honey looks down at her.

HONEY

No.

Marty looks at the corpse, surprised.

MARTY

Not dead? Pretty fucked up though.

HONEY

Not a client.

MARTY

Oh. So whatta you here. At a traffic fatality.

HONEY

Whatta you.

MARTY

Whatta I what.

HONEY

Homicide detective. At a traffic fatality. How come.

MARTY

I'll tell you if you tell me sumpn.

HONEY

Shoot.

MARTY

Shoot, like shit? Or shoot, like go ahead?

HONEY

Shit, Marty, you talk like an obstacle course. Shoot. Go ahead.

MARTY

Okay, well, you're unattached. Why won't you see me socially?

HONEY

This is social. She's not a client.

(*turning to go*)

And Marty, I like girls.

Marty guffaws.

MARTY

Aw, you always say that.

CONCRETE BUMPER

The parking-space bumper is stenciled, RESERVED O'DONAHUE. A car pulls in with a hot stop.

Match-cut to the rear of the car as its rocking settles. Its vanity plate: HONEYDONT.

The bottom of the driver's door swings open and legs emerge.

Looking up: low on Honey straightening as she gets out. High behind her is the signage for this low-rent strip mall. The biggest sign is for GENERAL YUM DONUTS.

STAIR TO HONEY'S OFFICE

Honey ascends the outdoor stairway toward a foreground door: HONEY O'DONAHUE and in smaller letters INVESTIGATIONS.

HONEY'S OFFICE

She enters the small reception area. Her assistant, Spider, sits behind the desk. One of the chairs in the waiting area is occupied by a perfectly put-together man in his thirties.

SPIDER

Mr Siegfried doesn't have an appointment. He's wondering if he could have a brief interview right now.

HONEY

Sure. You can cancel tomorrow's appointment with Mia Novotny. Come on in, Mr Siegfried.

SPIDER

Should I charge her for the canceled appointment?

HONEY

She didn't cancel. She . . . withdrew. Tell you later.

INNER OFFICE

Honey sits in behind her desk and gazes across it. A beat as she looks, frowning.

The man is using his handkerchief to wipe the facing chair. He wipes the seat, wipes the arms of the seat, curls the wipe carefully around the arms' scrolled ends, and responds to Honey's look as he seats himself:

SIEGFRIED

Covid.

HONEY

Okay.

SIEGFRIED

Please don't look at me that way.

HONEY

What way am I looking at you.

SIEGFRIED

In a judgmental and supercilious way.

Her look is neutral.

HONEY

Sorry. How's this.

Her inexpressive look holds. Beat.

SIEGFRIED

I think my boyfriend is seeing someone.

HONEY

I'm sure he is.

Siegfried's face falls. His look to Honey is vulnerable.

SIEGFRIED

How do you know?

HONEY

Nobody ever comes in here saying that, when everything's okay. Want my opinion?

Siegfried does not have a quick answer and Honey plows on.

. . . I'm a private investigator but on a first interview I do advice for the lovelorn and it's free. Either ignore the affair or bring it up with your boyfriend in a non-hostile way. Wine and flowers. Honest discussion. Honest about each other's needs, desires, so forth. The one thing you don't want to do is pay me a hundred bucks an hour to learn something we both already know.

A beat as Siegfried absorbs this. Finally he shakes his head.

SIEGFRIED

No, I have to know.

HONEY

I'm saying, you do know.

SIEGFRIED

I have to know specifics – who, where, when. I have to be able to rub it in his face. Rub it in his lying bastard face.

Honey sighs.

CAR

Honey drives. A highway-side billboard advertises the Four-Way Temple. The minister, pictured in a robe, is a forty-year-old man wearing tinted glasses: Reverend Drew Devlin. The billboard proclaims, 'It's Priceless. It's Free. It's God's love. Come on in.' The Four-Way Temple logo is familiar from the ring of the dead woman in the overturned car: four faceted triangles pointing out from a central sphere.

TRAILER PARK

Honey's car pulls off the highway into a sunbaked trailer park.

TRAILER INTERIOR

Honey's pregnant sister, Heidi O'Donahue, stands at the stove. She stirs a large pot of pasta while bouncing a small child, Alan Jr., on her hip. An eight-year-old boy, Dizzy, storms Honey when she enters.

DIZZY

Honey Honey Honey Honey Honey.

He runs a tight circle around her, one extended hand tracing her waist as he circles.

HONEY

Hello Dizzy.

HEIDI

Hi Honey, you want some mac 'n' cheese?

HONEY

Already had lunch.

HEIDI

This is dinner.

HONEY

I'm fine. I brought some grapefruits.

HEIDI

Thanks, but the kids won't eat it. They won't eat anything that isn't yellow.

HONEY

They're yellow.

HEIDI

The outside is yellow.

DIZZY

Honey, will you marry me?

HONEY

I can't marry you, Dizzy, you're not old enough.

A bellowing male voice from elsewhere in the trailer:

VOICE

Where's my charger?

DIZZY

When I'm older will you marry me?

HONEY

Can't even then, there's a law against it.

DIZZY

What's the law?

Thumps and crashes.

VOICE

Who took my charger?

HONEY

People can't marry their aunts.

DIZZY

Why?

HONEY

Because our kids would be your sons and daughters, but they'd also be your nephews and nieces and it gets too confusing.

DIZZY

I could keep track of it, I promise I'd keep track of it, I love you, Honey.

A door bangs open.

HONEY

I love you too, Dizzy, but we can't break the law.

DIZZY

We could hide. We could live in the woods.

HONEY

There aren't any woods. Not a strip of shade between here and Bakersfield.

HEIDI

Don't talk down where he lives.

HONEY

I'm not, I'm just saying there're no trees. Heidi, do you ever feed them fresh fruit?

HEIDI

I feed them what they'll eat. Parenting is not rocket science.

Dizzy grabs a grapefruit.

DIZZY

I'll eat it, Honey.

She intercepts him as he bites down.

HONEY

Let me peel it for you.

(*to Heidi*)

I'm sorry. Yes. Nobody should tell you how to parent.

A sixteen-year-old boy is stomping in: Larry, Jr., heavily acned.

LARRY JR.

Did you take my charger, you snot-snivel?

HEIDI

Don't call your brother that. And say hello to your ont.

LARRY JR.

My *ont*?

DIZZY

She meant ant.

LARRY JR.

Shut up, snot-snivel, are you a mind reader?

We hear another door bang open. A male voice:

VOICE

Everyone shut up. I'm trying to sleep.

A fifteen-year-old boy stomps in: Steve, Jr.

HEIDI

If you got in before three in the morning you could sleep at night. Say hello to Honey.

FEMALE VOICE

You didn't wash the *sheets*!

HEIDI

I didn't have *time*!

A seventeen-year-old girl enters with an armful of sheets: Corinne. She has a punky look – green in her hair, green lipstick.

CORINNE

Mom.

HEIDI

I didn't have time. *You* can wash them.

DIZZY

Oh god! Blood! Blood!

CORINNE

Me!

HEIDI

Yes you, Corinne, you can –

DIZZY

Are you *okay*? What happened to Corinne?

STEVE JR.

She's menstruating, dingdong.

HEIDI

It's just a condition.

DIZZY

A *condition*? Oh my *god*.

HEIDI

She's fine, Dizzy, all women menstruate.

DIZZY

Oh my *god*. *You* don't menstruate, do you, Honey?

MINUTES LATER

Heidi and Honey sitting on the stoop – a one-step concrete slab shaded by a small vinyl awning – drinking coffee. Heidi holds a stuffed envelope.

HEIDI

If it's a girl her name'll be Mariella. If it's a boy it'll be Darryl Jr.

HONEY

What do Steve Jr. and Larry Jr. think about that?

HEIDI

They don't even notice the siblings they already have.

HONEY

And you want another one?

HEIDI

Don't tell me how to parent!
(*shakes the envelope*)
If you think this buys you the right to –

A car grinds up in front of the house, honking and sending up dust.

HONEY

That's just to help. I'm not telling you *how* to parent. I'm asking how *many* you're gonna parent.

Corinne bangs through the trailer door behind them, slipping a couple things into a pocket in her purse. A fumbled item drops between Honey and Heidi. Honey quick-catches it – a green-capped lipstick tube – and hands it back up to Corinne, who skips down the steps.

CORINNE

Thank you, NeeNee.

Honey smiles but Heidi wears a parent-frown:

HEIDI

Home by midnight.

Corinne is climbing into the car:

CORINNE

I'm not coming home tonight.

The door slams and the car peels out. It recedes to quiet.

HEIDI

Don't say anything.

HONEY

I didn't.

Honey's look drifts off, away from confrontation.

. . . Haven't said a word since we were kids.

FEMALE VOICE

You are the light!

DREW DEVLIN

He is having doggy-style sex with a busty young woman. Her call-outs are dutiful not passionate:

YOUNG WOMAN

Yes. You are the light. Yes. You are the –

DREW DEVLIN

Hold it lower.

He is referring to a mirror, which she holds two-handed on the mattress in front of her.

YOUNG WOMAN

It won't go lower.

DREW DEVLIN

Tip it lower.

She does.

. . . Not that much! The point is for me to see your bosom – jouncing – while we have fellowship.

She adjusts it. He resumes his action.

YOUNG WOMAN

Yes. You are the light. Yes. You are the light –

DREW DEVLIN

Tip it left.

YOUNG WOMAN

. . . Your left or my left?

DREW DEVLIN

(*explosive*)

We're facing the same way! Goddamnit!

YOUNG WOMAN

(*snippy*)

I'm sorry, Reverend Drew, you aren't being clear, should I –

A loud rap at the door.

DREW DEVLIN

What!

Shuggie, a muscled man in a sleeveless tee, opens the door.

SHUGGIE

Reverend, I was driving up with a shipment with Little Joey and all of a sudden he starts frothin' at the mouth like a fuckin' rabid dog, like a –

DREW DEVLIN

Whuh whuh whuh wait. Stop. Big Little Joey or Little Joey?

SHUGGIE

Junior. Little Joey.

Drew Devlin carefully disengages from the young woman who blandly listens to Shuggie's account.

DREW DEVLIN

Uh-huh.

SHUGGIE

So he's frothin' at the mouth like Mr *Bubble* and then all of a sudden he stops frothing and screaming and he's, he's . . . he's dead.

DREW DEVLIN

He's dead.

SHUGGIE

He's dead.

DREW DEVLIN

This is where?

SHUGGIE

Cab of the truck.

DREW DEVLIN

Yes and WHERE'S THE TRUCK, SHUGGIE?

SHUGGIE

Oh, we were, I dunno, just north of Long Beach, thereabouts, and I finished driving here, didn't know what else to do quite frankly.

DREW DEVLIN

. . . Is he still dead?

Shuggie is nonplussed. After a beat:

SHUGGIE

Ye— What do you mean, Reverend?

DREW DEVLIN

I mean, I think he's still dead. That's my guess. And that's not going to change.

SHUGGIE

No, Reverend.

DREW DEVLIN

So why did you have to interrupt this?

Shuggie looks at Drew Devlin and then at the woman and for the first time registers the situation.

SHUGGIE

Oh. I'm sorry. I apologize, miss. Should I – come back –

Drew Devlin has been wiping himself with a towel. He now tosses it aside.

DREW DEVLIN

Forget it, I'll come out.

GARAGE

A burly old man is sobbing as he applies CPR to an unresponsive body laid out beside a truck.

OLD MAN

Joey! Joey! Joey!

Drew Devlin approaches from behind. He lays a consoling hand on the man's shoulder.

DREW DEVLIN
(*gently*)
He's gone, Joey. He's gone.

OLD MAN
NOOO! No, *Joey*!

He grabs up his son's body and hugs him, rocking, sobbing. Drew Devlin addresses Shuggie who, in deference to the bereaved, is standing with his hands clasped in front of him and his head cast down.

DREW DEVLIN
Was he using our matter?

SHUGGIE
. . . Huh?

DREW DEVLIN
Did he OD.

OLD MAN
Joey! Uh-HUNGH! Joey! Joey! Uhh-HUNGH!

SHUGGIE
Oh. Yeah. Guess so, OD, yeah, lotta snot 'n' drool.

DREW DEVLIN
Did you know he was using? Using our matter?

SHUGGIE
Nah. Not till he started gettin' all, *wet*, and, spastic.

DREW DEVLIN
Because it wasn't his to use. It's the Temple's.

SHUGGIE
Yeah, course.

Drew Devlin bounces a finger toward the dead man:

DREW DEVLIN

This is *God's* will. It is *God's* punishment.

SHUGGIE

His will be done.

DREW DEVLIN

And if I for one minute suspected that *you* were using the matter . . .

Big Little Joey has struggled to his feet still holding his dead son. Drew Devlin's speech grows absent as he watches the old man start to shamble off, clasping his son to himself.

. . . doing it with him, taking our matter, our church's matter –

SHUGGIE

Nah, not my style, Reverend, my body's a temple, you should see me with the shake weight.

DREW DEVLIN

What the hell is he doing?

OLD MAN

Joey! Joey!

Reverend Drew and Shuggie watch the old man recede. At length:

SHUGGIE

He parked at the Walmart.

SUNBAKED BAR SIGN

The sign is not lit, it being day. Its neon shows two champagne glasses with ghost positions tipping toward each other to clink.

We hear faint piano music from inside the bar.

INSIDE THE BAR

Honey enters out of hard sunlight. The piano music bumps up at the cut inside.

The piano is inside a horseshoe-shaped vinyl-bumpered bar and is being played by a woman in her forties with piled-high hair.

HONEY

Hello Elle. Gary around?

ELLE

He says he is. How ya doing, Honey, ain't seen you in a while. Didn't go and get sober, did you?

HONEY

I wouldn't do that.

ELLE

And don't. First step on a slippery slope – stop drinking – start exercising – have sex with men – vote Republican . . .

Her lazy chording has morphed into a piano-bar arrangement of 'Honey Don't.'

. . . Take it from me, Honey, I been there. The lost years . . .

A kitchen door bangs open and Gary – a man in his forties – enters, wiping hands on a towel.

GARY

Honey O'Donahue, ain't seen you in a minute. Want a drink? Noon somewhere.

HONEY

No thanks. Can you tell me anything about this woman Mia Novotny?

GARY

Well I was pretty angry at her when she didn't show up for her shift Tuesday. So when I find out she's dead, well, that's a pretty good excuse for missing work. So *I'm* the dope.

HONEY

Uh-huh.

GARY

I'm a dick, mad at a poor dead woman.

HONEY

People can always find a way to put you in the wrong.

GARY

Yeah and dead people, the worst. Sure you don't want nothing?

HONEY

Do but I can't right now. Was she working here long?

GARY

Hardly nothin' at all. A week. Why, she owe you money?

HONEY

No, never even met her. She called me, said she was afraid of someone the cops couldn't help her with. We were supposed to meet here today, after her shift.

GARY

Well, ya can't help her now.

HONEY

Yeah, I feel lousy, she called for help, I said I'd help.

ELLE

You couldn't have helped her real problem: taking curves too fast.

HONEY

(*dubious*)

Uh-huh.

ELLE

Uh-huh, what. Cops said it was an accident.

HONEY

Uh-huh.

GARY

I don't know what to tell you. Lived in Delano, about all I know.

HONEY

You sleep with her?

GARY

Me? No. She was a little too pleasant, I don't like a positive person. Smiled, ya know.

He imitates her smile, perhaps pleasant in the original but grotesque on him.

ELLE

Nice ass though.

GARY

Yeah. Give her that.

GLITTERING WATER

Hard sun makes dazzling points on the water surface. Music: German electronic pop.

The mysterious woman we saw at the crash site sits on a chaise at the pool of a desert motel. Beside the chaise is a music player, source of the Kraut-techno-type music. A swivel-arm tabletop is swung out over the woman's stomach and on it is a ledger and next to the ledger is an ashtray. The woman wears a green sun visor and examines the ledger, a pen in one hand hopping down the ledger lines, her other hand holding a cigarette from which she occasionally takes femininely debonaire puffs.

A creak of the pool-area gate: Drew Devlin enters with an attaché case. He puts the case down in front of the woman – who has not looked up – and plants himself in front of her, hands on hips. The only sounds are lapping water and the music.

Drew Devlin's look leaves the woman to take in the bleak arcade of rooms and the brutal sun.

He looks back down at the woman. He smiles.

DREW DEVLIN

You don't have to stay here when you come up. You could stay at my place.

The woman still hasn't looked at him. She lets the invitation dangle for a good beat, takes a drag on the cigarette, and then, sadly, suavely, and still without looking up:

BRUNETTE

Mmmm-*non*.

Drew Devlin nods, not surprised. It was worth a shot. After a nodding beat:

DREW DEVLIN

Everything okay?

Another beat. Then:

BRUNETTE

Oui.

She closes the ledger with finality and then fetches up the attaché case and opens it and sorts through the cash inside:

. . . But zay are not hep-pee, *les peuples*.

DREW DEVLIN

(*uncomprehending*)

Who's not happy?

BRUNETTE

Les peuples.

DREW DEVLIN

. . . Oh! Well – why not? We're doing well, we're all doing well.

(*a jut of his chin at the money*)

They're getting their share.

BRUNETTE

Zay sink we are doing not so good may-be. We are going to be doing more better wiss someone else, may-be. Someone who makes fewer people dead.

DREW DEVLIN

Jesus Christ, that wasn't my fault!

BRUNETTE

Dead people brings police, et ceter-ah. Zay don't care about 'fault.'

DREW DEVLIN

Someone happens to die in some accident that had nothing to do with our business – that's not gonna spoil *my* day. Haven't lay poop-luh ever heard of God's plan?

A chinging *noise as she flips him something small and metallic. He catches it: the ring from the woman in the car. As he turns it over, gazing at it, he conciliates:*

. . . I do appreciate your helping. And this means there won't *be* no police et ceter-ah.

The woman snaps the attaché case shut. As she stubs out her cigarette:

BRUNETTE

I will tell zem 'God's plan' but I don't know. Zay are Fraunsh. Very sec-u-lar.

HONEY

Threading between the desks in a police station house.

VOICE

Honey O'Donahue!

It is Marty Metakawitch, the detective from the crash site. He looks up from his desk, beaming.

. . . Twutta we owe the onna?

HONEY
That woman in Antelope Canyon.

MARTY
Dead one?

HONEY
There was only one.

MARTY
Yeah and the coroner confirmed she was PFD.

HONEY
Huh?

MARTY
Pretty fuckin' dead. I remember you didn't have an opinion.

HONEY
Nobody pays me for an opinion dead or not.

MARTY
Nobody pays me for an opinion is that chick hot or not. You doing anything tonight?

HONEY
Book club. Do you have an address for her?

MARTY
The dead girl?
(*picks up phone, hits three digits*)
I like books.

HONEY
(*skeptical*)
What was the last book you read, Marty?

He stares at her for a beat.

MARTY
. . . What wuzzat one? . . .

(*attention goes to phone*)

Hey, MG, will you give Honey our address on Novotny, that dead girl in Antelope Canyon? . . . Yeah, thanks.

(*hangs up*)

What's your connection, you never said.

HONEY

No, I didn't.

MARTY

Uh-huh. Okay. MG's got the address. Lemme know if you find anything. She lived with her mother. Mother's a pain inna ass. She won't tell you nothin'. It's a traffic fatality. Speeding on the curve. I don't know why you don't like me. I'm a good guy!

CORRIDOR

Low angle looking down a linoleum hallway. Tap-tap-tap-tap – *Honey's high heels enter in the foreground and she crops in as she recedes, heading for a cage window in the background.*

On MG – a handsome, uniformed female cop – behind the cage window, waving a slip of paper.

MG

Address you wanted.

HONEY

Thanks, MG.

MG

Any time, Honey O'Donahue. Love those click-clacking heels.

Honey, heading away, looks back with a half-smile.

HILTON GARDEN BAR

Colligan, a man in his early thirties, well-groomed, slick-casual, gets the bartender's attention.

COLLIGAN

Cinnamon schnapps?

The bartender nods and starts pouring. The man watches, nodding.

. . . Got a date.

BARTENDER

Mm-hm.

COLLIGAN

. . . Don't want my breath smelling.

BARTENDER

Mm.

A Latino man of about twenty – Hector – walks up.

HECTOR

Mr Colligan.

Colligan gives him a glance that takes in his socio-economic status, and he is dismissive:

COLLIGAN

Yeah.

Colligan smiles wryly at the bartender.

. . . *This*. Is not the date. Believe me.

BARTENDER

Mm. Here you go.

He puts the cinnamon schnapps in front of Colligan.

HECTOR

Mr Colligan, I got your order.

COLLIGAN

Thank you.

Nothing happens.

. . . Well? Can I have it?

HECTOR

You suppose to pay me. And for the last order.

COLLIGAN

Fuck's sake.

With civility, turning to the bartender:

. . . I'll be right back.

With no civility, to Hector:

. . . Let's go outside and discuss this, friend.

HILTON GARDEN PARKING LOT

The lot holds only a few scattered cars, no other people.

COLLIGAN

Look. I have a tab. This is not a street deal.

HECTOR

I don't know nothin' about that. I'm suppose to get money for it and they said for same amount before, you didn' pay.

COLLIGAN

What are you, the accounting department?

Hector stands mute.

. . . Acch. Listen to me. I have a date. This is for a party. I'm busy. Can I please have the order.

HECTOR

I'm suppose to get money.

COLLIGAN

Hello, do you speak English? I don't have the money on me!

Hector stands mute.

. . . Okay look. I don't have time to argue but I think we can work this out. Just, let me have it, and I'll pay next time I order, and for right now I'll suck your cock.

Hector looks confused.

To make it right.

Hector doesn't understand.

. . . Okay?

Colligan drops to his knees and reaches for Hector's fly.

Hector looks down, horrified, frozen, but when his zipper is pulled down he unfreezes, shoves Colligan.

Colligan, surprised, looks up, off balance. He shoves back.

COLLIGAN

Bastard!

Another shove from Hector. Some messy pushing back and forth, as Colligan gets to his feet, ends with Hector punching Colligan. He collapses backward to the pavement.

Hector looks down. This is bad.

Colligan, spreadeagled on his back, woozily raises his head, his nose a mess, blood down the lower half of his face.

Panic. Hector runs for his car.

INSIDE THE BAR

The bartender, hearing engine roar and the squeal of tires, inclines his head to get a view out the window.

His point-of-view: a car is screeching backward out of its parking space and bumping over something on the ground, something hidden by the crop of the window. The car is thrown into drive and bumps again over the unseen obstacle. But as the car recedes toward the exit what it ran over comes into view: Colligan, whose leg has somehow tangled in the rear bumper so that his limp body is now being towed.

The bartender watches, horrified.

The car makes a hot turn into the street. Colligan's body, swept around by the turn, smacks against a sign stanchion with a reverberant clung. *It detaches from the car and rolls to stillness as the car speeds away.*

HONEY DRIVING

A straight-ruled desert highway.

She sees, oncoming:

A motorcycle. Something unusual about its rider.

It's a woman wearing white short-shorts, a horizontal-striped sailor crop top, sunglasses, and a commodore's cap.

It is the Frenchwoman, and she passes Honey without a side-glance, bike roaring, hair whipping like a pennant.

SEEDY DESERT-COMMUNITY STREET

Old tract housing, houses set back on dead lawns.

Honey raps at the screen door of one of them.

A middle-aged woman materializes in the dark beyond the screen door.

MAN'S VOICE

Ask if it's collection. They gotta say if it's collection.

The woman hesitates, hand on the door, looking at Honey. She projects:

MRS NOVOTNY

It's a woman.

MAN'S VOICE

They can be women.

HONEY

I'm not collecting anything, I don't want money. Your daughter called me the day before she passed away.

The woman stares at her.

MAN'S VOICE

. . . Who is it?

The woman pushes the screen door open with a creeeeak.

KITCHEN

A minute later. Honey is seated across the table from the woman and an unshaven man holding a can of Schlitz. On a counter behind Honey a cat eats from a tin can that rattles as the cat licks.

HONEY

You don't know why she might have called me?

MAN

Hell no. She don't know.

HONEY

. . . Ma'am?

MRS NOVOTNY

. . . I really don't. Who calls a private detective, somebody got a cheatin' spouse or what, I don't know. Mia didn't have no spouse 'n' no steady, I don't know, I truly don't. Detective, that is the craziest thing, someone in this family callin' a detective, that's like callin' the cable company when y'ain't got cable, why on earth would you do such a thing.

MAN

Told you. She don't know.

BEDROOM

Honey hesitantly enters Mia's neat bedroom. Its late inhabitant's effects are all still in place. Mrs Novotny lingers at the doorway, watching.

Honey looks at poetry-magnet words that have been stuck to a metal board over a desk:

selfloveworth

Honey looks down, picks up the paperback on the nightstand: The Self-Esteem Workbook.

MRS NOVOTNY

She read them self-help books.

Honey opens to a random place as Mrs Novotny natters querulously on:

. . . I think it was that *car*; she was a good driver. I think it was Mal. Function. She had just brought it in for Mal Function, had to leave it at the shop 'n' ride the *bus* into town.

Most of the two facing pages are highlighted in yellow. A turn of the page. The new page is entirely highlighted. So is the facing page. A flip through the rest of the book: almost all the text is highlighted. The flipping-by yellow text is broken up only by the occasional flash of unmarked white.

. . . We do not ride the bus. We are not cheap Christmas trash. You ride the bus, Ray?

MAN

Hell no. I *drive*.

Honey's attention is drawn away from the book by a cat mew and the patter of feet. She looks down.

The bed next to the desk, the cat just disappearing under it. There's a bit of white fabric on the floor there, peeking out.

MRS NOVOTNY

We *drive*. We do not ride the bus. Well they told her the car was fixed and give it back to her but your mechanic will take advantage of you, that's *widely* known.

Honey squats, reaches in, pinches the fabric to draw it from beneath the bed. It is a simple short-sleeved white robe.

MRS NOVOTNY

That was for her church in town, don't know a which a one she went to. She didn't wear that in the house.

The light cotton garment has something inside that weights it. Honey gives the shoulders of the robe a little bounce and what's inside thumps to the floor: underpants with metal studs at the waist and a cut-out crotch, and a brassiere with cut-out cups.

MRS NOVOTNY

Them neither.

DREW DEVLIN

He is at a pulpit, wearing a simple short-sleeved white robe like the one we just saw.

DREW DEVLIN

But Action ungoverned is not action in the service of the Lord: Action must be connected to Submission. Submission is not passive. And Action is not unbridled. Only in submitting – vigorously! – to the will of God, do we serve Him!

Shouts of 'Amen!' The congregation too wears the white robes.

We Submit – and yet we Act! We Act – and yet Submit! Even to the desires of the body we Submit, Actively, and so serve the Lord!

'Amen!'

Now you all know what a piece of macaroni does. What does a piece of macaroni do?

'Sits there!'

It just sits there. And is that macaroni serving the Lord?

'No sir!' 'Not hardly!'

We are not macaroni! We serve the Temple through Action! We serve the Temple through Submission! We do not serve the Temple by sitting there like macaroni!

'Shame on the macaroni!'

Now you all know what the Pharisees were. The Pharisees were the high and mighty – so they thought! They knew the laws right down to the letter, and that made them holy – so they thought! They knew right, they prayed right – but did they Act right?

'No sir!'

And what does that make them?

'MACARONI!' The verdict is thunderous. Drew Devlin nods, approving.

The Pharisees were macaroni. Duty. Passion! Action. Submission! Those are the Four Ways!

'Amen!' 'The Four Ways!'

. . . Those are the only Four Ways!

'Ain't no other way!' 'Amen!' 'Ain't but the Four!'

And in serving our Temple – doing our Duty – Passionately! – Acting – Submissively! – we serve the Lord. And we serve his minister. And there is no higher service!

SACRISTY

Drew Devlin is frozen with his robe not quite hoisted off, still on one shoulder, one hand still clutching it. He stands in a white jockstrap, staring.

At length:

DREW DEVLIN

But – he's such a nice boy!

Shuggie, the muscled goon from earlier, shrugs.

Drew Devlin stares, still not able to make sense of it. He gives up, finishes taking off the robe, reaches for a pair of pants.

. . . What did he say happened?

SHUGGIE

I think the guy he was sent to collect from made some kind of . . . penis move.

DREW DEVLIN

. . . A penis move.

SHUGGIE

Some move that, uh – that was against Hector's, his, his code of machismo.

DREW DEVLIN

Okay.

SHUGGIE

I couldn't really get a description out of him. He was very upset.

DREW DEVLIN

Upset! I guess he was – if the other guy is gunked up in his tire treads.

SHUGGIE

We cleaned his tires. Cleaned his whole car.

DREW DEVLIN

Okay, but, that doesn't make the dead guy go away.

SHUGGIE

No. Yeah. Most of him was still in the parking lot.

DREW DEVLIN

The French are not gonna like this!

SHUGGIE

. . . The French?

DREW DEVLIN

Don't worry about it. I mean, *you* don't gotta worry about it, above your pay grade. But *I* gotta worry about it. Be*lieve* me.

SHUGGIE

We don't know anyone'll connect Hector to it.

DREW DEVLIN

No one saw Hector and the guy?

SHUGGIE

Only the bartender.

DREW DEVLIN

Okay, well, we gotta kill him.

SHUGGIE

Okay. Wow. Okay. Well. I'll find out where he lives.

DREW DEVLIN

You don't know where he lives?

SHUGGIE

How would I know where he lives?

DREW DEVLIN

. . . Hector?

SHUGGIE

. . . We're talking about Hector?

DREW DEVLIN

Who do you think we were talking about?

SHUGGIE

The . . . the bartender?

DREW DEVLIN

THE BARTENDER! WHY THE FUCK WOULD WE KILL THE BARTENDER!

SHUGGIE

He – he – saw . . . Hector –

DREW DEVLIN

And he's talked to the police! That ship has sailed! Dingbat!

SHUGGIE

Oh. Okay. So . . .

DREW DEVLIN

Too bad. I liked Hector.

HONEY'S OFFICE

Mr Siegfried is there again, weeping, head down. He gropes blindly toward the desk with one hand.

Honey, behind the desk, is momentarily puzzled – then realizes what he's reaching for. She yanks two Kleenexes from a box on the desk and puts them in the reaching hand.

The hand retreats and Mr Siegfried blows his nose into the Kleenex and sets it aside and gropes some Purell from his bag.

HONEY

I'm so sorry for your loss.

Mr Siegfried squeezes Purell onto one hand with a goop-fart splurt and rubs it into both hands.

Honey's hand slides under the lip of her desk and presses a button. We hear it buzz faintly in the outer office.

. . . It seems you were right, the bartender says your partner had a date. Though it wasn't with his . . . assailant –

Spider enters.

SPIDER

Your appointment with the Gramercys?

HONEY

Oh yes. Right.

Through tears:

MR SIEGFRIED

They don't know who did it?

HONEY

No. They have a physical description.

MR SIEGFRIED

And they don't know – you don't know – who his – his – his date was with?

HONEY

To be honest I hadn't started working on it. I don't think there's any point pursuing that now, is there, Mr Siegfried?

A look from Honey to Spider, who coaxes Mr Siegfried up with a hand to his elbow.

MR SIEGFRIED

I don't know! I just don't know! I just don't know!

HONEY

I think it's best if we let . . . sleeping dogs lie. But I'll let you know if there's any progress on the police investigation of your partner's . . . passing.

Mr Siegfried is fully up but still weeping. Honey tries to be helpful:

. . . Perhaps you have a friend, or, or, a clergyman who can . . . help you grieve?

He shoots her a vicious are-you-kidding look. Honey appeals to Spider with a look and Spider manages to get him out the door.

Honey turns to a Rolodex and flips through cards. Many of them are stamped in the upper right with an icon of a battleship canted at 45°, sinking beneath the waves.

She finds the right place in the alphabet but flips back and forth, stymied: no card for the person she seeks.

Spider has stuck her head back in and has been watching.

SPIDER

I could make you a, you know, database? Computers?

HONEY

No, I've got a system. Could you get me a number for MG Falcone, I don't have her.

SPIDER

Just call the precinct.

HONEY

Personal number.

SPIDER

. . . Do you ever just go home and read a book?

HONEY

Number.

AN OLD WOMAN

An ancient cholita in Bolivian bowler hat is threading chillis onto a string.

HECTOR

(*off*)

Abuela!

OLD LADY

Sí!

Hector enters. In Spanish, subtitled:

HECTOR

I'm going to church, where's my robe?

OLD LADY

Hanging, I did the wash. It's dry now but I haven't ironed.

HECTOR

I'll bring it in.

The woman strains to get up.

OLD LADY

You don't need to bring it in, I'll bring it in.

He puts a hand on her shoulder.

HECTOR

I'll bring it in, Grandma.

OLD LADY

It's laundry, it's woman's work.

HECTOR

You work too hard, Grandma.

OLD LADY

It's woman's work!

He pats her shoulder, leans in to give her a kiss.

HECTOR

I love you, Grandma.

OLD LADY

Of course. But laundry is woman's work.

OUTSIDE

A 'backyard' which is no more than an enclosed patch of desert. On a line, laundry billows: a white robe and several brightly colored shawls and dresses. It is quiet but for the murmur of desert wind and the flap of fabric.

Hector placidly hums. The white robe before him, animated by the wind, blocks our view of whatever might be behind it.

Hector reaches for the clothespin high to his right. Just as he is about to grab it, a gust of wind flaps the robe, dipping the line, making him miss the pin.

HECTOR

Heh.

He corrals the line with his other hand to steady it, then reaches again for the pin. He carefully pinches it.

The pin scissors instead of opening. It still holds the robe.

. . . Eh.

Hector reaches one hand to each shoulder of the billowing robe and –

– snaps down, freeing it from the line, exposing endless desert beyond.

Hector resumes humming.

The wind abates, the clothes have less motion. Hector proceeds to the next hanging garment, a shawl, yanks it from the line, drapes it over an arm. He goes to the next shawl, yanks it, drapes it over an arm; goes to the next . . .

TRACKING TOWARD THE HOUSE

Hector leads us, the laundry draped over one arm.

He slows short of the door, looking down.

On the ground in the doorway a bowler hat wobbles.

Hector drops the laundry –

HECTOR

Abuela?

– and runs inside.

KITCHEN

The old woman lies on the kitchen floor, her colorful skirt and shawl fanned out, her eyes staring sightlessly up. Her throat has been slashed.

HECTOR

Abuela!

He wails and kneels and gently takes her chin in his hand and tips her head toward him.

. . . Abuela!

In her glassy eyes a reflection of Hector and, behind him, movement.

Hector tucks and rolls away as Shuggie completes a downward knife-slash that misses Hector and ends with the knife planted in the old woman's chest. Her open-weave shawl snags the knife and slides off her body when the knife is withdrawn.

SHUGGIE

Sorry, mate! Not my idea! I just work here!

He's trying to work the knife out of the shawl when Hector yanks the shawl away from him and barrels him into a counter.

Hector opens the cutlery drawer just at his hip and with his other hand slams Shuggie's head into it face-down. The silver jangles.

Hector slams the drawer with all his might on Shuggie's forced-down head – once, twice, cutlery clanging, Shuggie howling.

An attempt at a third slam fails when the drawer is yanked open too far and disengages and dumps its clattering contents. Hector flings the drawer away.

Shuggie straightens, hands pressed to his boxed ears and his own screams distanced by the pure ringing inside his head, which we hear sympathetically.

Shuggie's screams are snapped off by his own Ulp! *as a fork slams upward to stick in his underjaw.*

Hector releases the fork and steps back, reaching for something, as Shuggie gropes for the fork and pulls it out of his jaw.

Just as Shuggie raises the withdrawn fork to see what it is that stuck him, a chunk of metal sweeps into frame and rakes his mouth. Blood and teeth spew sideways.

Hector dumps the bashing implement – a flat iron – and plucks Shuggie's knife from the dropped shawl. As he steps in for the

kill, Shuggie burbles blood from his mouth and underjaw and reaches one hand round to the small of his back.

As Hector plants the knife in Shuggie's chest, Shuggie's hand is coming back round with a gun from his waistband. BOOM! he fires point-blank and Hector flies back and lands with a crash and there is silence.

Shuggie, whimpering, turns away with the knife still in his chest. He kneels, blubbering, to the silverware on the floor. He swipes through it, his jaw-dribbled blood and the spray from the chest-lodged knife making it hard for him to pick out his little white teeth.

His whimpering stops when the flat iron sweeps down to smash his head to the floor. Hector, clutching his gun-shot belly, slams the iron down twice more to cave in Shuggie's skull.

HECTOR

Abuela!

We stay on dead Shuggie as Hector drops the iron and leaves frame. When he re-enters he's holding the gun, which momentarily wavers since Shuggie's disassembled head offers no obvious target for coup de grâce. *But whatever: Hector fires, then again, and again, wailing:*

. . . Abuela!

BAR

Honey steps in and pans the crowded blue-collar cop bar.

MG is sitting at the bar. Honey goes over and takes a vacant stool next to hers.

HONEY

How's your day?

(*to the bartender*)

Tequila and . . .

(*head shake*)

Just tequila.

MG

Oh, the usual. Listening to people complain, waiting for five o'clock. Yours?

HONEY

Slow.

The crush of bodies at the bar has forced them close and they have swung to face each other. MG's left arm rests on the bar. Honey matter-of-factly takes it and puts it below frame. MG's reaction to whatever this gesture is, is minimal.

HONEY

. . . Not much doing at work. Had a cheating-spouse case but the spouse got killed. Case before that, client died.

MG

The woman in Antelope Canyon?

HONEY

Yeah.

MG

No more client, why go to her house?

HONEY

Nothing else to do.

MG

You don't have hobbies?

HONEY

You mean like . . . step-dancing? Do you?

MG

Have a hobby? Yeah.

HONEY

Wuddya do.

The two women are focused, deadpan, on each other. MG's arm is lightly jogging.

MG

What do I do. I knit.

HONEY

You knit.

MG

Yeah. Right now I'm knitting . . . the Periodic Table of the Elements. To hang on the wall.

HONEY

Because you might forget one. You want a reference. On the wall.

MG

That's right.

Honey's speech is now slow and a little breathy:

HONEY

On the wall . . . is not knitting though. That's, crochet.

MG

Crochet . . . is a kind of knitting.

HONEY

No, actually. Crochet is . . . crochet.

MG

I love first-date stuff. Hobbies . . . Turn-ons . . . Turn-offs . . . Your trip to Cancún . . .

Honey's breath is more and more uneven. Her eyes are locked on MG's and there is a strangely focused beat, neither person moving aside from the jog of MG's arm.

Honey breaks the silence.

HONEY

Come here a lot?

MG stares at her.

MG

Fridays.

More beat, more intent staring, more minuscule action. At length:

. . . I like it. They leave you alone.

HONEY

Nn.

MG

. . . What was the case?

Honey takes her time answering.

HONEY

. . . Dead girl's case?

MG

Mm.

HONEY

. . . Never found out.

VOICE

Another?

The bartender has paused on his way past. MG's look swings to him.

MG

Nah.

Honey has also turned her head to the bartender. Her mouth is open, her eyelids heavy.

HONEY

We're ready to go.

The bartender raps the bar to acknowledge and moves off. MG's look returns to Honey and she eases back on her stool. Honey breathes.

. . . Before we get arrested.

MG raises her hand from below the bar and casually licks one finger and, still looking at Honey, uses it to stir her drink.

MG

For getting to know each other?

WOOOF!

Honey has slammed face-first, palms bracing, against a wall. She is naked. MG, her shirt hanging open, is behind her and grinds into her.

MG withdraws from Honey and grabs her by the shoulders and turns her and presses against her, front-to-front now, kissing hard, as Honey reaches up to push MG's shirt off her shoulders, push sleeves off arms, fling shirt away, both women now naked.

Sex and struggle with Honey finally pushing away from the wall and the two women land –

– on Honey's bed, Honey on top. More kissing and then Honey rises to her knees and goes headboard-ward to press her innermost self into MG's face.

MG's arms come up and push on Honey's shoulders to flop her backward and MG's head rises. She pivots forward and down and with both hands pressing Honey's thighs she seeks the center of all being. Honey both wants, and doesn't want, to have MG tow her waterskiing to the end of the universe and send her crashing through its far wall. She gropes back at her nightstand.

She claws and roughly opens its drawer and withdraws handcuffs.

Honey pushes MG onto her back and grabs a wrist and slaps on a bracelet.

MG

Who's the cop here?

Honey slaps the other bracelet onto the headboard.

KITCHEN SINK

Next morning. Rushing water. We hear humming. Honey's hands enter with a large dildo. It gets washed and . . . vigorously shaken and . . . set in the dish rack.

Honey's hands return to the sink to wash – an even larger dildo, an even brighter color.

Shaken off, set in the dish rack.

Now a long, long string of anal beads. Just as Honey starts washing it – DING-DONG.

Honey's look comes up from the sink. The classic housewifey gesture: she raises a soapy hand and with the back of her wrist brushes a wisp of hair from her forehead. Her look off says, Who could that be?

FRONT DOOR

Honey opens it to her niece, dressed for work in her fast-food uniform but whimpering, with her head cast down.

HONEY

Corinne?

Corinne looks up. Her face is badly bruised. In combination with the green hair and green lipstick, the bruises make a dismal picture.

IN THE APARTMENT

Honey is sitting at a table kitty-corner from Corinne, carefully dabbing antibiotic on with a Q-tip.

CORINNE

I couldn't go home, Aunt Honey, Mom'd freak out and say I told you so, she hates Mickie so much.

HONEY

Yeah it sucks when your mother's right.

MG, leaning against the bedroom doorjamb, smoking a cigarette, hoots.

MG

Doesn't happen much.

CORINNE

But I don't need to hear it from *her*.

HONEY

Your boyfriend beats you up and I'm not gonna tell your mother?

CORINNE

NO! YES! She's in my shit so much already!

HONEY

She isn't in your shit enough.

CORINNE

She just yells at me, Honey – *look* at me, I need *support*, I don't need *that*! Please, Honey, why does Mom have to know, she'll just yell and call the *cops*!

Honey and MG exchange a look.

MG

Cops already know.

HONEY

MG's a cop, Corinne. They don't all look like Tom of Finland.

CORINNE

Oh god! Oh my god!

(*an appeal to MG*)

We don't have to make it official, do we? Mickie doesn't mean anything by it, he loves me, he just gets in these . . . moods.

MG rolls her eyes, blows out smoke.

MG

Your face didn't get pushed in by a mood, honey-doll. But suit yourself.

(*shoves off from the doorjamb*)

I gotta get dressed.

HONEY

Sweetie, I *should* tell your mother. But I won't – if you promise not to see that creep again.

CORINNE

Yeah, no, I won't, of course I won't!

MG's voice, through the open door of the bedroom:

MG

She's lying.

Corinne projects, defensively angry:

CORINNE

No I'm *not*!

We hold on Honey's look, weighing whether to believe her.

ROLODEX CARD

It's for MG FALCONE. We hear the dull thunk of a stamp against an inkpad and then the stamp enters frame to thunk the card, printing on it the battleship at 45° sinking beneath the waves.

Honey, in her office, fits the card back into the Rolodex.

SPIDER

She put up a fight?

She's handing a piece of paper across the desk to Honey.

HONEY

Just the right amount. What's this?

SPIDER

The white robe you asked about. That's who sells it, that's who buys it around here.

HONEY

'Four-Way Temple.'

SPIDER

Here's their address.

HONEY

Seen their sign. 'God's love is free.'

SPIDER

You like free love, dontcha boss?

HONEY

Not with *God*. I'm not a pervert.

FOUR-WAY SANCTUARY

It is empty. From elsewhere in the building, a male voice:

VOICE

Active Submission! Active! Not macaroni!

SACRISTY

Close on Drew Devlin, lying face-up on a bed. The ass of a woman bounces up and down, slamming him against the bedsprings. The woman faces away from him, her calves tucked back on either side of his head. The shins of another woman are on either side of this woman's calves, this second woman apparently straddling the first. The four legs are a chaos of driving impetus and flailing response.

The bottom woman wears a metal-studded jockstrap. So does the woman she hugs, facing her, rocking in rhythm with her and amplifying the up-and-down motion.

Both women are gasping. Though Drew Devlin is being helplessly chest-slammed and bounced, he seems to be in charge:

DREW DEVLIN

All right, Cara! Now, you slide toward me, and submit yourself, actively, to my mouth! And you, Brandi, you come back with her . . .

The girls waddle awkwardly backwards, trying to comply while maintaining their humping. Drew Devlin is dissatisfied:

Don't lose the sacred contact, Brandi! Through Cara, you will feel my –

BANG – the door bursts open.

HECTOR

YOU KILL MY ABUELA! YOU KILL M— huh?

Hector stops mid-stride, shocked, raised gun frozen.

The threesome on the bed is likewise shocked and frozen. The two women take a goggling beat, planted like a contortionist act, the lower woman on her knuckles and knees, the higher woman on the lower –

DREW DEVLIN

Hector! Not in the sacristy!

– and now the women scream and unfreeze, reacting to the gun, frantically trying to disentangle from each other and from Drew Devlin, the six arms and legs complicatedly getting in each other's way.

Hector raises the gun-hand to shield his sight from so many body parts.

HECTOR

I'm sorry, miss! I'm sorry, miss!

Screaming women, a swirl of bedcovers and bodies. Drew Devlin grabs one woman by the shoulders and holds her facing out as a shield.

DREW DEVLIN

Think about what you're doing, Hector! These girls haven't done anything to you!

HECTOR

Get away, miss!

He waves at her with the gun, still only half-looking, respecting her modesty.

DREW DEVLIN

Think about it, Hector! They're just like your abuela!

This is too much for Hector. He shrieks, charging the bed, one hand still shielding his eyes but the gun now pointed.

HECTOR

Don't you talk about my abuela, cojudo, I kill you a thousand times!

The girls redouble their screams and give up trying to cover themselves. They launch from the bed. Hector is free to look now and he fires! and fires! and fires!

But nothing is beneath the disarranged sheets, the bed he shot at is empty, and –

WHACK! Hector is struck down from behind by a heavy candlestick.

Drew Devlin drops the candlestick and stoops for the gun. He rises, carefully sights down.

We see him fire but are spared the sight of Hector's death – the one sad moment in this movie.

Drew Devlin's look holds on Hector below frame. After a beat, he mournfully shakes his head, looks up – and shows irritation.

The women are hugging each other in a corner, whimpering, strap-on dildo wobbling between she wearing it and she formerly harboring it.

DREW DEVLIN

Big help you were.

WIENER HEAVEN

Long-lens point-of-view of a man sitting at a Formica table in a sparsely occupied fast-food restaurant. He is seedily dressed, in his sixties, stubbled, clothes hanging off him. He has long acquaintance with hard times.

His bloodshot eyes are directed at the camera. He stares, sadly open-mouthed.

After a beat the camera slides laterally to lose him from view.

On Corinne, easing away from her peek out into the restaurant from behind its counter. Next to her is another girl in uniform.

CORINNE

He's still there.

OTHER GIRL

So what?

CORINNE

He's been there for three hours. With one cup of coffee. Who comes to Wiener Heaven for the coffee.

OTHER GIRL

He's like, homeless.

CORINNE

And creepy.

(*into a microphone after a glance at a screen*)

Welcome to Wiener Heaven may I take your order?

There is a squawk. Corinne frowns.

. . . A what?

PROCESSED VOICE

A second, I said gimme a second, I'm looking at the . . .

A long beat.

. . . I'll have a . . .

A longer beat.

CORINNE

Take your time, sir.

Corinne turns to the other girl.

. . . He still there?

OTHER GIRL

Quit asking!

CORINNE

Just look!

The girl cranes to look out.

Her sliding point-of-view brings in the old man who, sensing movement, looks quickly and expectantly up.

Seeing who it is, he isn't interested. His gaze drifts back down to his coffee.

Corinne's colleague draws back.

OTHER GIRL

He's just homeless. He isn't creepy.

PROCESSED VOICE

Okay I'll have the, uh . . . I'll have the combo.

CORINNE

Which combo, sir.

PROCESSED VOICE

. . . The wiener combo?

CORINNE

They're all wiener combos, sir.

CHURCH OFFICE

Drew Devlin sits with one elbow on his desk, holding a business card, which he stares at for a long beat.

Finally:

DREW DEVLIN

. . . What the fuck!

Another beat. Still staring at the card:

. . . What the fuck!

He drops the card and his look shifts and the three words are now interrogative:

. . . What the fuck?

A new henchman – Pork Chop – stands before him. He shrugs, disclaiming any knowledge of what the fuck. Drew Devlin insists:

. . . The fuck she want?

Pork Chop shrugs again.

PORK CHOP

Talk to you. Is what she said.

DREW DEVLIN

About what?

Pork Chop shrugs again. A beat.

PORK CHOP

. . . Should I tell her to fuck off?

DREW DEVLIN

NO! *You* don't tell people to fuck off! Above your pay grade! *I* tell people to fuck off! *You* wanna run the church? People would love that! Love to hear *your* fucking sermons, Pork Chop! Hear *your* thoughts on divinity. Are you fuckin' kiddin' me? Know who you are! *Know who you are!*

PORK CHOP

Okay, boss.

He awaits instructions.

After a beat:

. . . So, should I –

DREW DEVLIN

You should shut the fuck up! While I think!

PORK CHOP

Okay, boss.

Pork Chop tries.

But he shifts, hesitates. He's been instructed not to talk, but his employer might want to know this:

. . . She's kinda hot, boss.

This interests Drew Devlin.

ON HONEY

Now seated in the office.

DREW DEVLIN

Mia! That's what it is!

Honey is puzzled.

HONEY

That's what what is?

DREW DEVLIN

Your interest. I wondered, what could possibly bring a private investigator to our little church.

HONEY

Well it's Mia Novotny. Did you –

DREW DEVLIN

Private investigator! Huh! And so attractive!

Honey considers this best ignored.

HONEY

Did you know her personally, have dealings with her?

DREW DEVLIN

Mia? Pastoral dealings, sure. Our congregation is large but not that large. I consider all of my dealings . . . personal.

HONEY

Uh-huh.

DREW DEVLIN

But I'm very puzzled, miss. Ma'am. Mizz?

HONEY

Just don't call me late for dinner. Puzzled why?

DREW DEVLIN

Heh heh! Well, because, it was a traffic fatality. Tragic thing, *terrible* thing, but – why is a private investigator looking into it?

HONEY

Who says I am? Looking into her death?

DREW DEVLIN

Isn't that what private investigators do?

HONEY

On TV maybe. What can you tell –

DREW DEVLIN

Do you drink?

Honey is momentarily taken aback. Then:

HONEY

Heavily, it's a point of pride. What can you –

DREW DEVLIN

Should you and I discuss this over a drink?

HONEY

No, this is business. What can you –

DREW DEVLIN

After business?

HONEY

Tuesdays I dry out. What can you tell me about her? Are you aware of any trouble she was in?

DREW DEVLIN

It's Wednesday.

HONEY

Today is Tuesday.

A beat.

DREW DEVLIN

. . . It *is* Tuesday.

HONEY

Can you help me, sir? Are you aware of any trouble she was in?

DREW DEVLIN

Mia was . . . in the same trouble we're all in. She was lost. She was seeking.

HONEY

She was 'seeking.' I'm not really after that kind of information.

DREW DEVLIN

You're talking to a priest.

HONEY

An unusual priest.

DREW DEVLIN

Not so unusual. I have a calling. I help people.

HONEY

Between drinks.

DREW DEVLIN

Judge not, Miss O'Donahue. You're fascinating.

HONEY

And you haven't even seen the riddle tattooed on my ass. This sex thing of yours, does it interfere with your calling?

DREW DEVLIN

Does yours?

HONEY

No, I keep the sex and the work separate.

DREW DEVLIN

Well *my* work is spiritual. It involves the whole person.

HONEY

Does it involve undressing the whole person? I've seen the women's wardrobe, it seems very different from the men's.

DREW DEVLIN

Women everywhere have wardrobe different from men's,
I thought we were talking about Mia. I *liked* her, miss.
A beautiful girl. I *like* people – I can tell that you don't.
I help people, I enjoy doing it. I see a need in people, I fill it.

HONEY

You see a need in people, you *exploit* it.

DREW DEVLIN

You don't know that. I see a need in *you* – to judge. I see you judging me right now, and that's all right, I forgive you. It's a way of shutting me out. I could help you with that – help you open yourself to other people. Why not open yourself and see what happens. You have nothing to lose but your fears.

She rises.

HONEY

Thanks, I'll stick with my dildo. It helps me open myself and it doesn't have a creep attached.

WIENER HEAVEN

We're looking past the dark foreground of the restaurant's tables, empty, at the bright background of the lit kitchen beyond the counter. The place is closed but we hear the clanks and clunks of clean-up.

CORINNE'S CO-WORKER

You got it?

CORINNE

Yeah, I'll lock up.

Corinne's co-worker enters from the depth, shrugging on a coat. She projects back over her shoulder:

CO-WORKER

See you tomorrow.

CORINNE'S VOICE

See ya.

The co-worker leaves. A beat. Clunk. Clank.

Corinne emerges from the depth, putting in earbuds. She flicks a light switch and stoops for a bag of garbage in the restaurant now dark.

A scream.

CLOSE ON MG

On all fours, facing the camera. The scream repeats. It's her.

MG

GAAAAAA!!!

She finishes her screaming orgasm and pants, sweating, finished but not yet moving. Whoever is behind her on the bed is hidden by her.

After a beat of her decompressing there is movement behind and she gives an ambiguous wince as we hear something

disengaging. It takes a moment, with MG giving a twist or two to facilitate.

Finally she seems to be at liberty and she rolls and drops onto her back, and we match-cut high looking down at her as she lands gazing up. Motion elsewhere on the bed. We hear a couple of thunks *of implements being set aside, then the click of a lighter. Honey drops in to lie on her back next to MG, holding a cigarette.*

The two women speak looking not at each other but at a point on the ceiling.

HONEY

. . . Didja see heaven?

MG

I saw . . . at least . . . Palmdale.

HONEY

Next time . . . we'll get you to Merced.

Honey runs one finger crosswise under her own lip, looks at it.

. . . Sorry, might've left some lipstick down there.

MG

S'okay. Only place I wear it.

MG still gazes up, contemplating the sex.

MG

. . . I don't usually do all that till a third date.

HONEY

I don't usually get to a third date. Next time we're off the map.

MG holds up a hand, fingers forked. Honey passes her the cigarette.

HONEY

Just tobacco.

MG

Mm-hm . . . Had a partner once lasted months, but . . . I had to end it. After sex she'd *weep*.

HONEY

Yeah I've had that. Why do they *weep*?

MG shakes her head around eyes still fixed on the spot on the ceiling.

MG

Never asked her. I knew whatever she said would piss me off.

HONEY

I guess they're looking for the whole smorgasbord.

MG

And you only want the one thing.

Her thoughts drift.

. . . My father used to hit me for my 'table manners.' Well he hit me all the time. God, *he* was a sonofabitch, always trying to beat *some*thing into me.

HONEY

He a cop too?

MG

Military. Same shit. War hero.

HONEY

How'd he deal with the lesbian thing?

MG

Never had to. Bought it overseas, being a hero. It would not have gone over well. Yours?

HONEY

Same. Not – sympathetic. He's still around though, somewhere. Looking for other people to fuck up I'm sure.

MG props herself on one elbow to look down at Honey. A beat.

MG

Let's do it again. Don't worry – I'll leave after.

CORINNE

Night. Walking, earbuds in, their cord trailing into the purse on her shoulder, one hand holding a compact mirror, the other applying green lipstick. Her head and body move to the beat of the music, which we hear only faintly leaking out.

A glance from the mirror up to the street as she walks.

Her point-of-view approaching a glowing bus stop. Street empty: it's late.

Back to Corinne, walking, attention split between mirror and the street. Now, though, a glance up – stays up. And her pace slows.

The bus stop's bench is coming into view as the angle clears it from behind the nearside panel. Someone's sitting, waiting, hands resting on knees.

Corinne slows further. A concerned focus of her look.

The person's body is now fully visible. An old man.

Corinne's eyes are on him just as he looks up: yes, it's the man from the restaurant. His look locks on her.

Corinne doesn't know whether to stop. Would it be rude – or prudent?

The man slowly rises.

The two stand twenty yards apart, staring at each other.

A bus cruises in to where the man waits. Brakes hiss, door opens.

The man doesn't look at it.

Corinne doesn't know what to do. Run to the door? He's right there.

A glance around, no help in sight. She decides: bolts for the bus –

– just as it gives up and moves away, door closing.

CORINNE

Hey!

But it continues on, and the man is still staring, and she's only closer to him now. She stops. The man doesn't move.

OLD MAN

I love you.

That does it: she turns and runs, green lipstick and compact clattering to the ground, lipstick tube rolling away clickety-click down the sidewalk.

CONCRETE BUMPER

It says RESERVED O'DONAHUE. A car squeals into frame and hot-stops.

VANITY PLATE: HONEYDONT.

CAR DOOR OPENING.

STOREFRONT DOOR yanked toward us.

COFFEE SPLASHING into a styrofoam cup.

STOREFRONT DOOR pushed out toward us.

HONEY'S OFFICE

Honey sits in at her desk with the coffee. Spider is leaning against the doorjamb.

SPIDER

Ya know I could make you coffee. Assistants do that.

HONEY

You're not an assistant, you're a poorly paid associate. And we don't begrudge General Yum his living. We all share this little mall.

This has been distracted: Honey is gazing at a photo she's lifted from the desktop.

It's Mia Novotny, holding her cat close to her face, smiling at the lens. A cute girly girl.

SPIDER

(*dry*)

Gee, I feel bad. I'll start buying bearclaws. How'd it go?

Honey's attention leaves the picture.

HONEY

The guy's a creep, maybe just a creep, maybe more than a creep. Wouldn't be surprised if this girl Mia called me because of the church, but I don't *know* that she did.

The phone on the desk rings. Honey reaches for it but Spider slaps her hand away.

SPIDER

My job. You sit and figure shit out.

(*into phone*)

O-D-I . . . Sure, Heidi, right here.

She gives the handset to Honey.

HONEY

What's up?

HEIDI'S VOICE

Have you heard from Corinne? I'm worried.

HONEY

Have I heard – today? No.

HEIDI

They called from work. She didn't show up, doesn't answer her phone.

HONEY

Well – when did she leave?

HEIDI

What?

HONEY

For work?

HEIDI

She didn't, from here. She wasn't home last night, she must've been at Mickie's.

Honey is distractedly pulling open desk drawers, ducking her head to peer into the depth, swatting things aside.

HONEY

Goddamnit, she promised me she wouldn't see him again, I'll go over there and –

HEIDI

Promised – *you*? *When?*

HONEY

I saw her – I'm sorry, Heidi, I should have told you I saw her, they had a fight –

HEIDI

Why did she go to *you*!

HONEY

She, I'm sure she just didn't want to get yelled at, I –

HEIDI

How could you *do* that, Honey, *you're* not her mother, now I don't know where –

Spider reacts to Honey's frantic search. She whispers:

SPIDER

What're you looking for?

HONEY

I'm sorry – Heidi – don't worry – I'll take care of this!

She punctuates by slamming the drawer shut and brandishing what she's just pulled out: a leather-strap-wrapped sap.

TRAILER PARK

Honey's car screeches to a stop in front of a trailer. A young man is sleepily coming out of its door, taking a step down, rumpling his hair.

Honey has popped her door and taken quick strides to meet him.

HONEY

Corinne here?

MICKIE

No. Who're you.

HONEY

I'm her aunt.

Without breaking stride, she raises one hand and stiff-arms him in the middle of the chest. It sends him stumbling backward into the trailer. She steps past him.

MICKIE

What the fuck?

TRAILER INTERIOR

As Honey enters, looking around.

HONEY

Just making sure.

MICKIE

How about you get back in your fuckin' car, lady, and –

He reaches for her and she parries the reaching hand and with her other hand swings the sap down at his nose.

His nose breaks and blood flows.

MICKIE

THE FUCK! WHO ARE YOU?

HONEY

I told you. Concerned relative. *Aunt*. When's the last time you saw her?

MICKIE

FUCK YOU! YOU CUNT!

He launches a fist. She slams the fist out of the air with the sap and grabs his raised hand, wrapping its fingers in her fist.

HONEY

Not 'cunt.' 'Aunt.' *A*. U-N-T. Every time you make me say 'aunt' I'm going to break something.

She punctuates by giving his fingers a hard twist. We hear a couple of them snap.

. . . What's the last time you saw her.

She puts a hand to his chest again and shoves. In the small space he comes up hard, against a gun rack. He turns toward it and starts to lift out a shotgun but it's awkward with his mangled hand.

From behind, Honey grabs a fistful of his hair and wrenches him sideways and sweeps a leg out from under him. He stumbles to the floor.

She takes down the shotgun, cocks both hammers, points the gun at him and arches an enquiring eyebrow.

With one hand covering his busted nose he looks up at the two barrels, at her, at the two barrels.

MICKIE

. . . Two days ago! Haven't seen her in two days!

HONEY

Haven't seen her since you beat her up?

MICKIE

YES! NO!

She stares at him for a beat, decides he's not lying. She eases the hammers down, breaks the gun open, shakes out two shells, closes the breach. Mickie flinches and covers as she swings the gun by its barrel, trying to smash the gunstock against the counter below which he lies.

Instead of the stock breaking, the cheap-shit counter dents.

HONEY

Goddamnit. Why do you assholes always have guns.

She heads for the door with the gun.

Her exit is followed, after a short beat, by dull thuds from outside. Mickie rises and goes to the door.

EXTERIOR

Mickie reaches the door, the thudding continuing. The last thud ends with a splintering sound.

Honey has just finished bashing the shotgun against the concrete-block support of one corner of the trailer. She strides back toward her car. As she passes Mickie she gives the gun an offhand toss his way.

He uses the hand not covering his nose to swat it defensively out of the air.

Honey flings open the door of her car – on the passenger side. She leans in, pops the glove compartment, and rummages.

She pulls out a sheaf which she leafs briskly through. She picks one item, tosses the rest back in the car.

Close on the back of Mickie's car. A faded bumper sticker: MAKE AMERICA GREAT AGAIN.

Honey's footsteps approach and her hand enters to cover that bumper sticker by slapping a new one on top of it: I HAVE A VAGINA AND I VOTE.

Honey gets back in her car and does a hot peel-out, clipping Mickie's side-view.

HONEY'S APARTMENT

Honey talks on her cellphone as she walks through the apartment toward its front door, responding to a knock.

HONEY

– Yeah, no, Corinne hadn't been there. I shoulda known. She said she wouldn't go there, I shoulda believed her – gotta know who people are. Hang on –

She reaches the door and flings it open to reveal –

– the old man from the bus stop, staring sadly in at her.

Honey, shocked, stares mutely back.

After a long beat:

OLD MAN

I love you.

Honey, staring.

A tinny voice from the phone forgotten in her hand. She raises it and responds to the voice, her eyes holding on the old man:

HONEY

. . . No, it isn't her. I'll call you back.

KITCHEN TABLE

Honey and the old man face each other across the table.

OLD MAN

I don't know how to say it . . . I'm just saying . . .

He works his mouth. Nothing comes out. He seems to be begging her to say something. She doesn't oblige. Finally:

. . . I want things to be different. Between us. Now.

This registers with no effect on Honey. After a staring beat:

HONEY

So . . . you don't want to beat me anymore.

OLD MAN

I never *wanted* to beat you!

HONEY

Well my mistake then – I apologize. Me, and Heidi, and Mom – we all thought you were *trying* to hit us.

OLD MAN

I'm sorry, Honey, I wasn't ready to be a father. Or a husband. But I am now! I've learned a lot about myself –

HONEY

A little late. Mom's dead.

OLD MAN

But I can be a father! And grandfather! I tried to talk to Karen, she just –

HONEY

(*puzzled*)

Who's Karen?

This makes him uncertain:

OLD MAN

. . . Heidi's . . .

HONEY

. . . Cor*inne*!

OLD MAN

Corinne, yes.

HONEY

When did you see her!

OLD MAN

Last night.

HONEY

Where, what did she say!

OLD MAN

(*despairing*)

Nothing, she ran away from me. Why would she run *away* from me!

HONEY

I don't know, Dad, sometimes kids are suspicious of old men who look like sex offenders.

OLD MAN

I never touched you that way!

HONEY

I said you *looked* like a sex offender.

OLD MAN

Why wouldn't she talk to me, why won't *you* –

HONEY

Where'd you see her?

OLD MAN

At her work, then after at her bus stop, she just turned and ran when she saw me. I only wanted to talk, I only want to talk to *you*, why are you so hard?

HONEY

Training.

OLD MAN

You're just hitting me back, Honey, that's not right either, you'll feel bad when I'm dead, if you leave it like this, when I'm dead you'll feel so sad, Honey . . . that you didn't let me connect with you . . . When I'm dead you'll feel bad . . . you'll feel so bad . . .

She watches him weep, hunched at the table.

HONEY

You're already dead. Hasn't anyone told you?

PANNING POINT-OF-VIEWS

Bakersfield street life. A lot of hard sun, not many pedestrians.

The points-of-view are Honey's as she drives, looking out. Dolorous music scores the montage.

Honey enters a vape store, a bodega, a cheap phone store, a mani-pedi shop, showing owners a picture of Corinne, getting only head-shakes.

Honey driving again. She pulls over, stops. Her look is on something across the street.

Her point-of-view: a bus stop. Cars whizz by in either direction between us and it.

On Honey, looking.

She gets out of her car, slams the door.

SECONDS LATER

Honey walks up to the bus stop's bench and plops down on it, thinking.

A vague look around, but the empty street doesn't hold any answers.

A hissing noise brings her look forward.

It's the airbrake on a bus pulling up in front of her, an advertisement on its side rolling into frame:

*'**Lost?** Discover the Four Ways to **Found** . . . Four Ways to peace . . . Four Ways to God.' Below the copy is a picture of Drew Devlin in a white robe.*

Honey stares at the ad for the Four-Way Temple, seeing something in it – or trying to.

Breaking the trance:

VOICE

Gettin' on, lady?

The bus driver has the door open, his hand on the lever.

She looks at him for a vacant beat.

He shrugs.

. . . Ya don't like this one? They're all pretty much the same.

He waits for a reaction. There is none. He closes the door and pulls out.

CLOSE ON A MESSAGE SLIP

It says, MARTY CALLED.

SPIDER

An hour ago. He asked for your cell.

Honey, entering the office, grabs the note.

HONEY

Oh god. You didn't give it to him.

She starts crumpling the note.

SPIDER

Course not. But he said it was about Mia Novotny.

Honey uncrumples the note.

HONEY

Make me a coffee, will ya?

INNER OFFICE

Honey sits in and smooths the message with the side of her hand. She reaches for the phone and dials.

SPIDER

What about General Yum?

HONEY

(*distracted*)

Fuck General Yum.

SPIDER

Okay, now I'm confused.

PHONE VOICE

Marty Metakawitch.

HONEY

Hi Marty, Honey O'Donahue.

MARTY

Hey doll. Can I call you right back, what's your cell?

HONEY

Sure, call me at the office.

MARTY

. . . Why can't I have your cell?

HONEY

Don't have one, I carry a bag of quarters for the payphone. You got something on the girl in Antelope Canyon?

MARTY

Yeah, ahh-right, be that way. Yeah, we got the coroner's report.

HONEY

And?

MARTY

Well, first of all he agrees this girl is dead. I remember you weren't totally sold on that.

HONEY

Uh-huh, and second?

MARTY

Well, you remember how tore up she was, it turns out 'some of the lacerations are not consistent with car crash.'

HONEY

What does *that* mean.

MARTY

She got stabbed and stuffed inna car I guess and –

HONEY

I know what it *means*, but what does it *mean*?

MARTY

I dunno, I'm not a deep thinker, but I will tell you that we had another stabbing homicide yesterday.

HONEY

A woman?

MARTY

Elderly woman, double homicide, other victim wasn't just stabbed, his head was all squashed to shit. But he had ID – some guy who works for a *church* if you can believe it.

HONEY

Four-Way Church?

MARTY

. . . How'd you know?

HONEY

I'm a detective.

MARTY

So'm I but I had to actually make a phone call to figure that out. Maybe we should, you know, get together, talk about detective things, compare notes – wuddya doin' tonight?

HONEY

Book club.

MARTY

That was three days ago.

HONEY

We meet a lot. Tough book. Dostoevsky. But I do appreciate it, Marty, you're my favorite . . . man.

She hangs up on his laughing 'Ah christ!' and stares at a point in space, hand lingering on the phone. Spider enters to put coffee in front of her. Honey speaks, still gazing off:

HONEY

If I don't know what I'm thinking . . . do *you*?

SPIDER

Do *I* know what *you're* thinking? Quite possibly. They're all eight balls on my mother's side.

HONEY

So, this girl Mia, I never met her, but I can picture her – a little lost, a little confused, a little fucked up.

SPIDER

Like Corinne.

HONEY

Corinne has more balls. But there's this guy who preys on the girls with less confidence, the sad ones, easy pickings.

SPIDER

The creep at the church. Your niece goes there?

HONEY

No.

(*her look has been off; it now goes to Spider*)

I mean, I wouldn't've *thought* so. But if you've been attacked, feel vulnerable, lost, they can't relate to you at home – where do you go? This church is sending out signals, 'Come here, come here, come here' – maybe if you've been hit enough times, you go there.

SPIDER

Maybe. Or maybe you go to a bar.

HONEY

. . . Yeah. Or maybe the mall or a movie or the roller rink. Still. Maybe.

FRENCHWOMAN

On her back on a mattress but up on her elbows, gasping, looking down her body.

FRENCHWOMAN

Oui! Bon! C'est bon! Okay! Now . . .

Drew Devlin looks up from her crotch, apparently having been giving her head. He submissively awaits direction. She urgently barks:

. . . Make love to me in the stupid American way!

DREW DEVLIN

. . . stupid American . . . You mean, like – *missionary* position?

FRENCHWOMAN

Yes! Yes! *Immediatement!* I am burning like a . . . how you say . . .

DREW DEVLIN

A . . . a . . . *fire*?

FRENCHWOMAN

Shut up, stupid American! Do eet! Do ze beezness!

Drew Devlin quickly elbows himself up her body and vigorously performs as instructed. She screams Frenchly with every thrust. Drew Devlin wears the expression of a boy given the run of a candy store, his ecstasy mingled with disbelief.

On a particularly loud French scream we cut to –

A MINUTE LATER

– Drew Devlin, hands clasped behind his head, gazing at the ceiling. He's satisfied, pleased with himself, can't quite believe his good fortune, but is still aiming to be suave.

DREW DEVLIN

That was amazing.

He looks to the Frenchwoman for confirmation. She is finishing getting dressed, ignoring him. He tries again:

. . . Best sex *ever*.

She doesn't look at him. Drew Devlin tries to bait her engagement with a compliment – not that it isn't genuine:

. . . Hot woman, knows what she wants.

Again no reaction. He props himself on one elbow, head on hand, examining her. She's indifferent to flattery, that's okay; he'll give voice to what he's been wondering:

. . . What made you change your mind? About me? About *us*? *Doing* it?

FRENCHWOMAN

Oh, I sought you should be able to comb one last time.

DREW DEVLIN

We . . . won't do it again?

FRENCHWOMAN

You weel not. Ze French, zey are not heppee.

BANG! She shoots him.

CHURCH PARKING LOT

On Honey, having just stepped from her car, hand still on its open door. She is frozen, reacting to the gunshot.

After a beat she slams the door, walks to the back door of the church. She tries it: locked.

Another noise: the start of an engine. It revs a couple times. Honey listens, trying to place the noise: from the far side of the church? She gives a quick last rattle at the door but her attention is drawn back to the noise as the vehicle is put in gear.

Grinding of gears. Honey tracks the sound, her head turning, as the vehicle downshifts, corners, re-accelerates.

The continuing engine noise briefly syncs with:

A motorcycle. It emerges from the church's side alley and we get a glimpse of the woman riding it before she corners and zooms away.

The motorcycle-roar fades.

Honey's look lingers, though. Something about the view holds her attention even with the bike gone.

Across the street and half a block down, is a bus stop.

MARTY METAKAWITCH'S DESK

He looks skeptical.

MARTY

Suspicious activity.

HONEY

Suspicious activity.

MARTY

You haven't described any suspicious activity.

HONEY

The gunshot.

MARTY

That's a noise. A noise is not an activity.

HONEY

Someone *firing* the gun would be an activity.

MARTY

If someone fired a gun. And it wasn't a car backfiring.

HONEY

'A car backfiring.'

MARTY

That's right.

HONEY

When's the last time you heard a car backfiring.

MARTY

What does that have to do with anything.

HONEY

'A car backfiring' isn't a real thing anymore. I didn't realize it was still a thing people *said*. Until you said it.

MARTY

I'm old-school.

HONEY

Maybe you should acknowledge what century it is.

MARTY

This from someone who uses payphones.

HONEY

I don't use payphones.

MARTY

AHA!

HONEY

Marty, okay, I'm – I'm *trying* to scratch your back. Remember how I'm supposed to scratch your back?

MARTY

Oh I remember.

HONEY

You find out what kind of hanky-panky is going on in this place, it's a feather in your cap.

MARTY

I bust into a house a' God for no reason, it ain't a feather in my cap it's my ass in a sling. Wudda you care, anyway? Why were you there?

HONEY

My niece is missing.

MARTY

File a report. What does she have to do with the church?

HONEY

I . . . I'm not sure.

MARTY

You're not building a strong case, Honey O'Donahue.

As she rises and stalks off:

HONEY

Fine! Forget it, Marty! Tried to help you!

MARTY

Wudda ya doin' tonight? After the book club?

TRACKING TOWARD MG

A reprise of the shot that introduced MG, low angle looking down the linoleum hallway toward her cage window in the background. Tap-tap-tap-tap – *Honey's high heels enter in the foreground and she crops in as she recedes, this time with urgency, heading for MG, who at the moment is turned away.*

Honey arrives.

HONEY

MG, is there any way you can –

She cuts herself off, surprised:

The person looking up from a file drawer is not MG but a young man.

YOUNG MAN

Can I help you?

HONEY

I – no, sorry, I was looking for MG Falcone.

YOUNG MAN

She asked me to cover her shift, I guess she partied last night. Something I can do?

HONEY DRIVING

Phone to her ear.

HONEY

Near Delgado, right? A couple blocks down?

SPIDER'S VOICE

That's right.

HONEY

How'd you get it?

SPIDER'S VOICE

Her address? Tried the gym nearest the precinct, said I was MG and I just lost my card and I –

HONEY

Okay, good work.

SPIDER'S VOICE

Why didn't you have it? I thought you two were, um . . .

HONEY

Never been there and she isn't answering her phone. Thanks, I'm almost there . . .

As she hangs up her look catches on something ahead.

Her point-of-view: a bus stop.

Honey's look swings to the side as she slows and draws even with it, then swings forward again as she resumes speed.

HONEY ARRIVING AT MG'S

She pulls into frame and stops at the curb. A distant hydraulic hiss catches her attention. She cuts the engine, reaches up to adjust the rear-view mirror.

Her point-of-view: a bus kneeling at the bus stop a block away. The bus hisses back up, trundles out into traffic.

On Honey. A thoughtful beat.

She looks at the home across the street, her look saying, Can this be the place?

Her point-of-view of the house. A little grander than one would expect for a public servant – or, once grand. Victorian, and now seedy. A little too big, a little overgrown.

FRONT DOOR

Honey walks up to it. She hesitates to ring the bell; the door's etched glass and the dark interior reinforce her dubiousness. Finally she rings. We hear a chime in the interior.

Out of its decay we hear a steady drip . . . drip . . . drip . . .

Honey slowly turns, her look finally placing it:

A drop hitting a floorboard on the porch.

Honey looks up from the drip to its source.

An overwatered potted plant is suspended from the porch ceiling. The plant has an exotic, fleshy flower, maybe the insect-eating kind.

The dripping sound continues. Close on a drop landing. The floorboard around the impact is discolored by the drips' long history. The toe of Honey's shoe enters and presses experimentally down: the floor is spongy with rot.

Honey goes to the door, gives two more short rings, grabs the doorknob and, after a hesitation, tries it. It turns.

Honey pushes the door open and steps in.

INTERIOR

Honey stands half-inside.

HONEY

MG?

From a distant room, but shrill:

VOICE

Mary Grace? Mary Grace?

Honey pauses, closes the door behind her.

PARLOR

Caged parrot in the foreground, Honey entering deep.

PARROT

Mary Grace? Wanna cuppa tea?

Honey drifts through the room, looking around at the worn 1970s furnishings.

There is a framed picture of a military officer. A framed picture of a young MG in a girls' Little League uniform. Older pictures, relatives.

Honey finds herself at a bookshelf. She scans the books, pulls down a hefty one, a yearbook: MOMENTS AND MEMORIES Sacred Heart School 2003.

Honey flips through the group and activity pictures, leafs through the senior's portraits, gets to the Fs:

Mary Grace Falcone –

The parrot squawks:

PARROT

Wanna cuppa tea?

– young MG in her school uniform, her hair big, her look elevated toward that place past the lens where graduating students see their future. But MG's burning look sees something unseen by the others. It's unsettling.

Her picture is captioned:

'ACTS Missionaries . . . Field hockey . . . Synchronized swimming . . . "God put us here to DO things, people!"'

The picture's spell is snapped by clunking noises, dull sound of feet on stairs.

HONEY

MG?

The feet-on-stairs ends with the creak of an interior door, then footsteps down a hall. MG enters, wearing sweatpants, holding a dusty toolbox. She stares at Honey. Honey meets her surprise with embarrassment:

. . . It was open, maybe I shouldn't've come in. I *rang*.

MG

Was in the basement, didn't hear.

(*indicates toolbox*)

Had to find this, cupboard door needs a plane.

She leaves with the rattling box, calling from off:

. . . I see you found my yearbook. They're always funny, huh?

Honey projects:

HONEY

Yeah. What you never want your date to see. Sorry.

MG

(*off*)

Quit apologizing. But why didn't you call?

HONEY

Did. Your phone's off.

MG

Is it? Oh – yeah. Oh. You called a couple times.

HONEY

It's my niece . . .

Honey wanders toward MG's voice and an accompanying sound of hammer-taps.

KITCHEN

Honey enters. MG is finishing tapping hammer against chisel against cupboard-door hinge pin, pushing it up and out.

HONEY

She's missing. I was hoping, maybe, you could help somehow. Unofficially.

MG's 'Uh-huh' is not enthusiastic. Her whole manner is slow, dull-eyed, defeated.

She eases the door off the hinges, exposing the cupboard's contents: many boxes of dried ramen and a stack of folded brown shopping bags.

MG sets down the cupboard door and looks at Honey, maybe daring her to comment on the ramen.

Honey tries to get it going:

. . . I know this is crazy but, she works at that hot-dog place on Irvine, and her bus stop to go home – well, she would have been there right around the time you were coming home. But. You didn't see her?

MG has been giving her a level look.

MG

No.

A beat.

HONEY

Something wrong?

MG

I was wondering the same thing. It's a little awkward, isn't it. You come to my place –

HONEY

Sorry, I tried to call –

MG

No, it isn't that. I know how this place looks. It's old.

HONEY

You don't have to –

MG

It's the house I grew up in.

(*puts the kettle on*)

My mother died when I was a kid, and I told you, my father . . . So with what I make I could either've rented a closet somewhere, or stayed here. I don't care, it doesn't define me.

HONEY

Listen to me. MG. I don't write for *ELLE Decor*. Who cares.

MG

Yeah, so you say, so you believe even. Kind of. But you were a little squirrely when I walked in.

HONEY

Sorry, I –

MG

Exactly – 'Sorry, sorry.' Ya think someone's hot, everything about 'em is exciting, then, second or third date they open their mouth, say something lame and – whoa, where'd *that* come from. I don't know this person at all, how could I have fucked *her*? Pussy Remorse – pretty hard to get rid of once it hits you.

(*looks around*)

Who the fuck would live *here*?

HONEY

No.

MG

Yeah, I'm pretty sure I saw Pussy Remorse, Honey. A little too much *Bakersfield*.

HONEY

And I'm a duchess? I'm from here too.

MG

(*not buying it*)

Uh-huh.

She shoves off from the counter as the tea kettle gives breathy stutters, approaching boil.

. . . Wanna cuppa tea?

Her going to the stove has cleared Honey's view of the counter by the sink. There are two teacups on saucers.

HONEY

Had company?

Both cups have tea-colored smudges on the rims where they've been sipped from, but one has a differently colored smudge as well.

Close on the cup as Honey rotates it to better see the smudge on its rim.

A loud squawk:

PARROT

Wanna cuppa tea?

The stuttering hisses of the kettle now become louder chirps –

MG

Yeah, I had company . . .

– the spin of the cup brings into view its smear of . . . green lipstick –

– the chirps of the kettle become a full boiling shriek and – WHAP! – a hammer smashes Honey's arm down.

MG screams along with the kettle:

> . . . A *sad*-ass!

She punctuates with another lunging swing of the hammer – this time of the claw-side. It misses Honey as she twists away and the claw lodges in the tabletop. The kettle shrieks on.

Honey's spin puts her facing away from MG, who sweeps a forearm under her chin and chokes her from behind while she hisses in her ear:

> . . . Anyone who *wants* to be a victim should get what they *want*. They're part of the problem. Anyone who *lets* her boyfriend beat her up –

Honey's balled fist shoots up past her own shoulder, thumb and thumbnail sticking out backward and aiming for MG's eyes. Two blind stabs.

MG eludes, but it makes her lose her chokehold on Honey. Honey spins to face MG, in the process swiping a knife off the tabletop.

MG, panting, glares at Honey:

> . . . That church girl, Mia? Just like your niece. Women who go to that church are nothing but *victims*. That place *advertises* for victims, come here, come here, let me fuck you, let me beat you. That's what she went for, *submission*, Honey. She *wanted* a beating. She *let* it happen.

HONEY

(*hoarse*)

Did *you*? *Let* your father beat you?

MG

Yeah but then I *didn't*, finally. I stood *up*. Decided to *do* something. That's a butter knife, Honey.

Honey looks down at the knife she holds – indeed a harmless-looking thing. A clatter brings her look back up.

MG is taking the top tray out of the toolbox. She sets it on the counter and pulls from the box's depth a shiny combat-ready knife. Not a tool for use around the house.

The parrot is loudly, non-verbally squawking, maybe overstimulated by the shrieking kettle, and the kettle finds an even higher, louder register of shriek, as if competing with the parrot.

MG projects over it all:

. . . This was Dad's. Wasn't really a war hero. He died standing right where you are. Stab wounds. A *lot* of stab wounds. Then I put him in the car, lit it up, the fire cooked it all away.

(*wide-eyed look around*)

This place is a fire trap. No sprinklers. Not up to code. Old and sad, isn't it, girlfriend? They won't look for stab wounds on you either.

Plink – Honey drops the butter knife.

MG lunges. As she stabs –

Honey twirls, reaching for something. Tremolo in the kettle shriek.

Honey completes her spin by slamming the kettle against the side of MG's head.

MG staggers sideways. Honey punches the kettle, bottom-side-first, into MG's face.

PARROT

Mary Grace? GAWWK!

MG flails backward, hits the floor. Honey reaches to her stomach with her free hand – staunching blood.

MG woozily props herself up with the heel of her left hand, right elbow and forearm against the floor with the knife still clenched in her right fist.

Honey stoops to punch the kettle down onto the knife-hand, squashing it against the floor like a sandwich press. Slosh-whistle from the kettle. A scream from MG.

MG reaches reflexively with her left hand to push the kettle off her burning right, and screams again, burning the left.

Honey straightens and backs away, leaving the kettle behind, both hands now to her stomach.

MG's scalded hand has lost the knife but she grabs the kettle handle with her left hand as she rises. Her face is seared. Blood streams from her scalp.

She advances on Honey, angling the kettle's bottom side at her, promising to do damage.

Honey backs blindly away and tangles in a chair on which MG's uniform coat is draped. She topples with the chair and then scrabbles in the mess on the floor and gets free of it and crab-walks away from the advancing MG.

MG

You're not part of the solution, Honey. You're a good fuck, but you're not doing SHIT, SOCIALLY!

She stoops for her coat on the floor and bats at it with her reddened right hand.

. . . You think they'll look for BULLETS in a SKELETON in the ASHES!

She has exposed her police gun belt which was hanging under her coat.

. . . In YOU – OR your FUCKING NIECE! *VICTIMS!*

She flips aside a bit of coat to expose the holster – empty.

She slowly straightens, puzzled. She looks at Honey, her smile fading, her face blistering, blood pouring from her hairline. She still holds the kettle.

BLAM!

A hole opens in the kettle and water hisses out.

BLAM! BLAM!

Two more holes open in the kettle. MG slowly lowers it, exposing three bullet holes in her chest.

As water escapes the kettle, its whistle withers away.

THUNK – MG drops the kettle.

BLAM!

MG, shot in the face, drops.

Honey, woozy, lowers the gun, rises.

Everything swims.

HONEY

Corinne . . . ?

LIVING ROOM

All is woozy as Honey staggers in from the kitchen, hand to her stomach. Her voice is weak:

HONEY

Corinne?

She grabs the standing birdcage for support but it doesn't help; it crashes to the floor with her as she collapses. The squawking parrot flies from the sprung-open door and screeches 'MARY GRACE?' as it bangs madly against the living-room window – twice – and drops.

BLACK.

FADE UP ON HONEY

Close on her face, gently rocking. At first, quiet.

Then, a childlike voice:

VOICE

Honey . . . ?

Honey slowly opens her eyes. Engine noise fades up. The voice repeats:

. . . Honey?

A siren fades up.

Honey's swimming point-of-view:

Corinne sits opposite in the back of the rocking ambulance. She looks disheveled and woozy. Heidi is hugging her.

The voice sounds again, and it is coming from neither Corinne nor Heidi:

. . . Aunt Honey?

Honey squints, puzzled. But now Corinne does talk:

CORINNE

Mom called your office. And found out where you were. And we were both there. That was weird . . .

VOICE

Honey?

Honey tries to process this. She's on her back on a gurney. And now someone is tugging at her sleeve.

She redirects her look, tries to figure out what she's looking at.

VOICE

Aunt Honey?

Her point-of-view: in the extreme foreground, leering in with concern, is Corinne's little brother Dizzy.

DIZZY
. . . Are you menstruating?

MARTY METAKAWITCH

We track in on him beaming, feet up on his desk.

MARTY
Honey O'Donahue! Twutta we owe the onna?

HONEY
Wanted to hear about the cold cases.

MARTY
We only found the two hookers so far. Might be all there is.

HONEY
Sex workers.

MARTY
Sex hookers, yeah.

HONEY
There was one in Palmdale . . . ?

MARTY
And another in Lancaster. Year anna haffago, and two anna haffago. Stabbings. We showed MG's picture around, people who knew these girls'd seen her. And yer gal in Antelope Canyon, that makes three stabbings.

HONEY
And MG's father?

MARTY
Fifteen-year-old ashes, who knows.

(*shrug*)

MG said she did it, we'll believe her. Honest cop. Hey Honey, you get the Cap inna Brainpan Award for that head shot – nothin' but net! Rightna fuckin' forehead!

HONEY

I practice in the bathtub.

MARTY

Yeah now yer fuckin' kiddin' me but I'm serious, 'at was a hell of a shot, sittin' position, stabbed, gushin' blood. Wuddya doin' tonight, Honey – I hope this hasn't put you off the entire department?

She is already turning to go.

HONEY

Don't know why you can't get it through your head, Marty. I like girls.

We are pulling away from Marty, still leaned back, hands behind his head.

MARTY

Aww, you always say that!

HONEY DRIVING

Nice day, top down, wind in her hair. She slows, stops at a traffic light. Waits. Idle hands – she turns on the radio. Old rock and roll.

A new sound: rumble of an unmufflered engine. The vehicle pulls up next to her, revs a couple times.

Honey looks over. The Frenchwoman on her motorcycle, waiting for the light.

The Frenchwoman looks at Honey. Eye contact. And then the woman's eyes travel, checking Honey out.

Honey notes it. Her eyes do the same.

A couple revs of the bike.

HONEY

Where ya goin?

FRENCHWOMAN

Airport. Plen to catch.

The accent, the look – it's intriguing.

HONEY

What's your name?

The woman smiles, shrugs, won't divulge. But then, okay:

FRENCHWOMAN

They call me Chère.

HONEY

'Chère.' That's like . . . Honey?

Sing-songy, French:

FRENCHWOMAN

More or less!

Another beat.

HONEY

What time's your flight?

The two women look at each other. A smile flickers back and forth.

BLACK.

The radio music goes direct, unfiltered, at the first chorus downbeat of 'Honey Don't.'